QUESTIONS AND

WONDERS OF THE OCEAN

WONDERS OF THE OCEAN

TEXT: MIKE BRUTON AND SUSAN MATTHEWS
TEXT CONSULTANT: CHARLES GRIFFITHS
ILLUSTRATIONS: DAVID THORPE

Contents

Introduction

The sea covers about three quarters of the Earth's surface, and so it is home to many plants and animals. Most live in coastal waters close to land, and provide us with food such as fish, mussels, perlemoen, rock lobsters and squid. Although the open ocean is much the same all over the world, the coasts are often very different. The north-east coast of southern Africa has coral reefs with colourful fish, while further south there are wide estuaries and long, sandy beaches where many sea creatures bury themselves under the sand. The rocky shores of the west coast have large colonies of seals and penguins that feed on huge shoals of fish.

The study of fishes is called ichthyology, and the study of the use and conservation of fish stocks is called fisheries science. Sea fishes serve as a valuable resource if they are carefully conserved. Each one of us can play a very important role in this conservation if we are well informed about sealife. By studying the animals and plants that we find in the ocean, on our beaches and in rock pools we can find out more about our fascinating sealife and discover the wonders of the ocean.

The sea

All living creatures in the sea are affected by the special features of seawater, such as its saltiness, temperature, tides and currents. By studying these features, we may learn more about life in the sea and on our beaches.

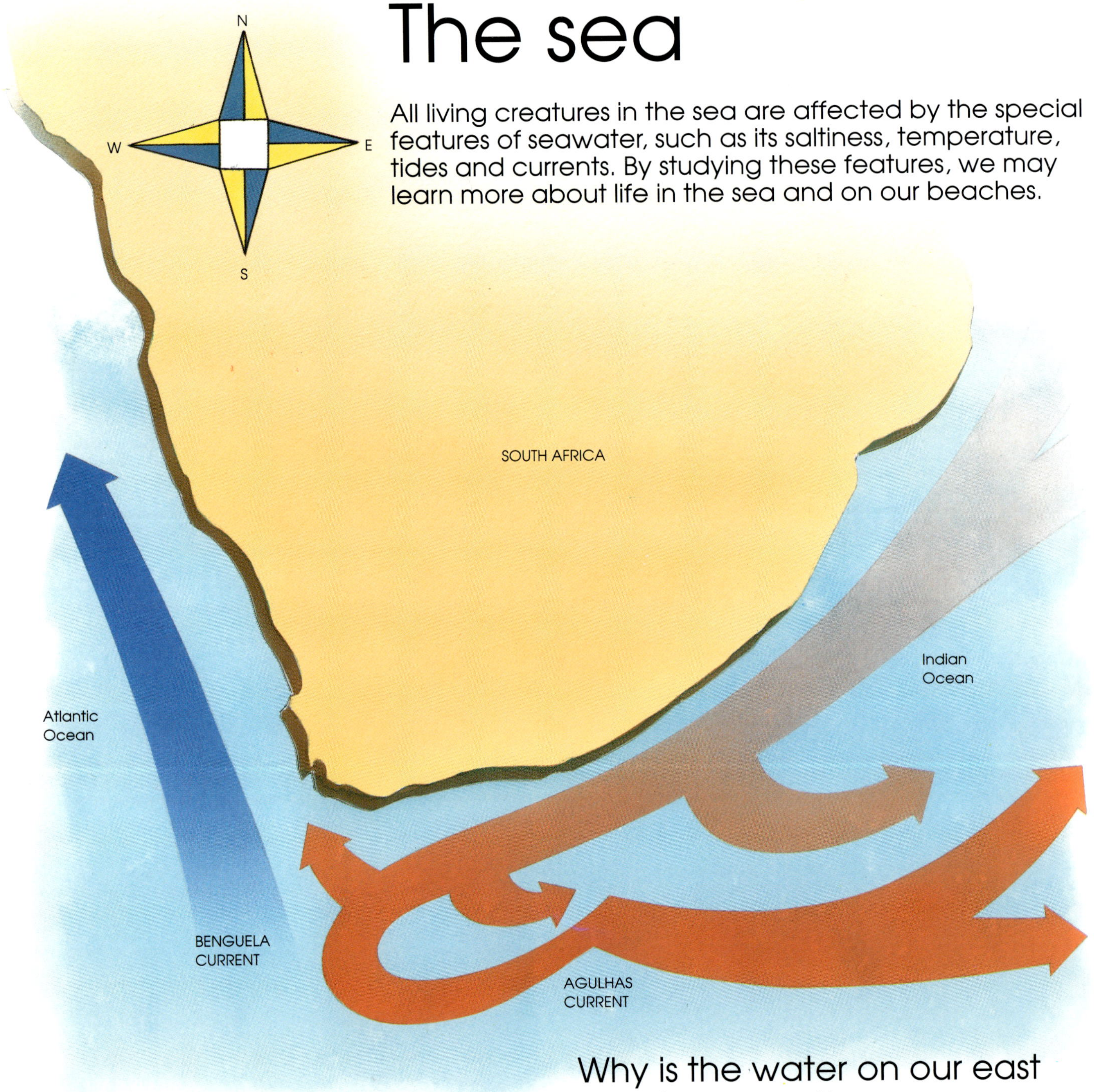

N
W
E
S
SOUTH AFRICA
Indian Ocean
Atlantic Ocean
BENGUELA CURRENT
AGULHAS CURRENT

Why is seawater salty?

It contains large amounts of two chemicals called sodium and chloride. The salt that we add to our food is actually crystals of sodium chloride that are left behind when seawater dries up. The amount of salt in the water is called its salinity. The salinity in the seas around southern Africa hardly changes at all, but in estuaries, where fresh water from rivers mixes with seawater, the salinity varies with the tides and how fast the river is flowing. Animals and plants that live in estuaries must be specially adapted to cope with these changes.

Why is the water on our east coast warmer than on our west coast?

The Agulhas Current flows southwards down the east coast, bringing with it warm water from the hot areas around the tropics and equator. This is an extremely powerful and fast-flowing current, and animals that get caught in it are unable to escape. Along the west coast, the Benguela Current brings cold water from the south and carries it northwards. The animal communities on the west and east coasts are very different, because some animals prefer cold water while others prefer warm water.

What is upwelling?

This is the movement of seawater from deep in the ocean up to the surface. On the west coast of southern Africa, surface water is blown out to sea by south-easterly winds in spring and summer. The cold, deep water below flows up to take its place. At first this water is very clear because no phytoplankton, the sea's tiny plant life, can live in the deep ocean as it is so dark. But this water is rich in nutrients because the animals and phytoplankton living near the surface sink when they die and release nutrients as they decompose. After a few days the nutrients in the upwelled water allow phytoplankton to grow and multiply rapidly, or 'bloom', and the water becomes murky and green.

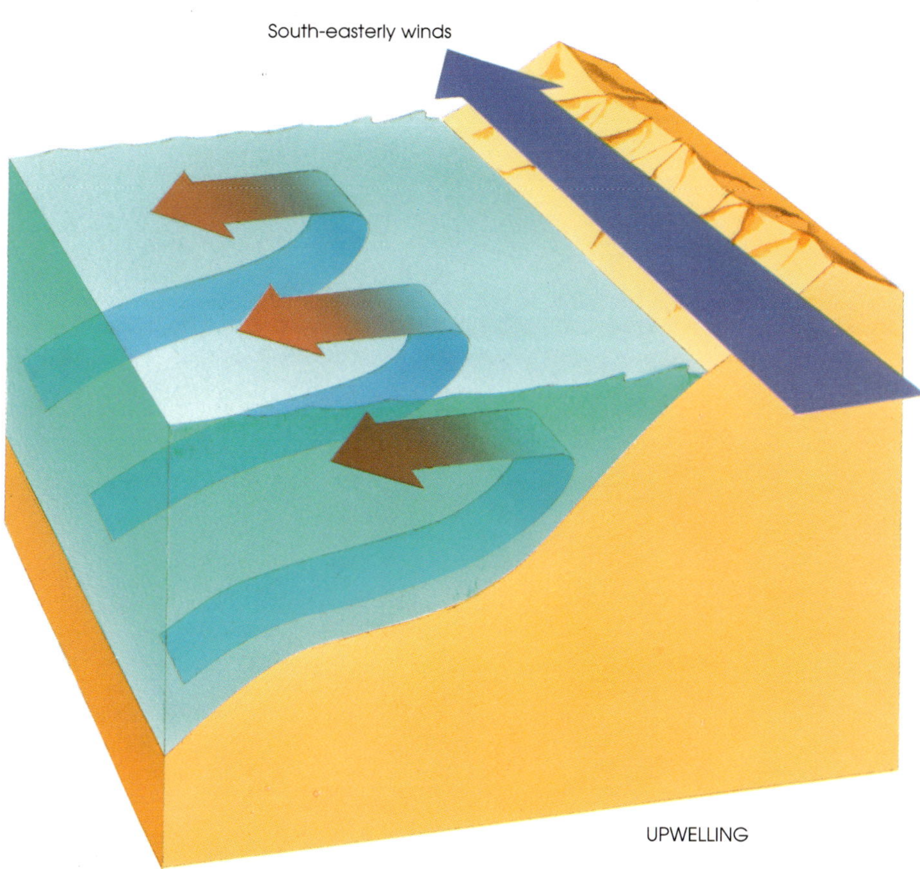

UPWELLING

Are tides affected by the moon?

Yes. Because of gravity, the moon pulls our ocean towards it, making it bulge out on the side of the Earth facing the moon. The ocean on the opposite side also bulges out as the moon and Earth spin round one another. These bulges cause high tides. As the water bulges out in these areas it is drawn away from other areas, causing low tides.

Do spring tides only occur in spring?

No. Spring tides are extra high and low tides that occur every two weeks throughout the year. They happen when the sun, moon and Earth are in line with each other. Their combined gravitational pull creates an extra large bulge of the ocean. Between the spring tides are neap tides, when high and low tides are smaller. These occur when the moon is at right angles to the sun, and their gravitational pull cancel each other out.

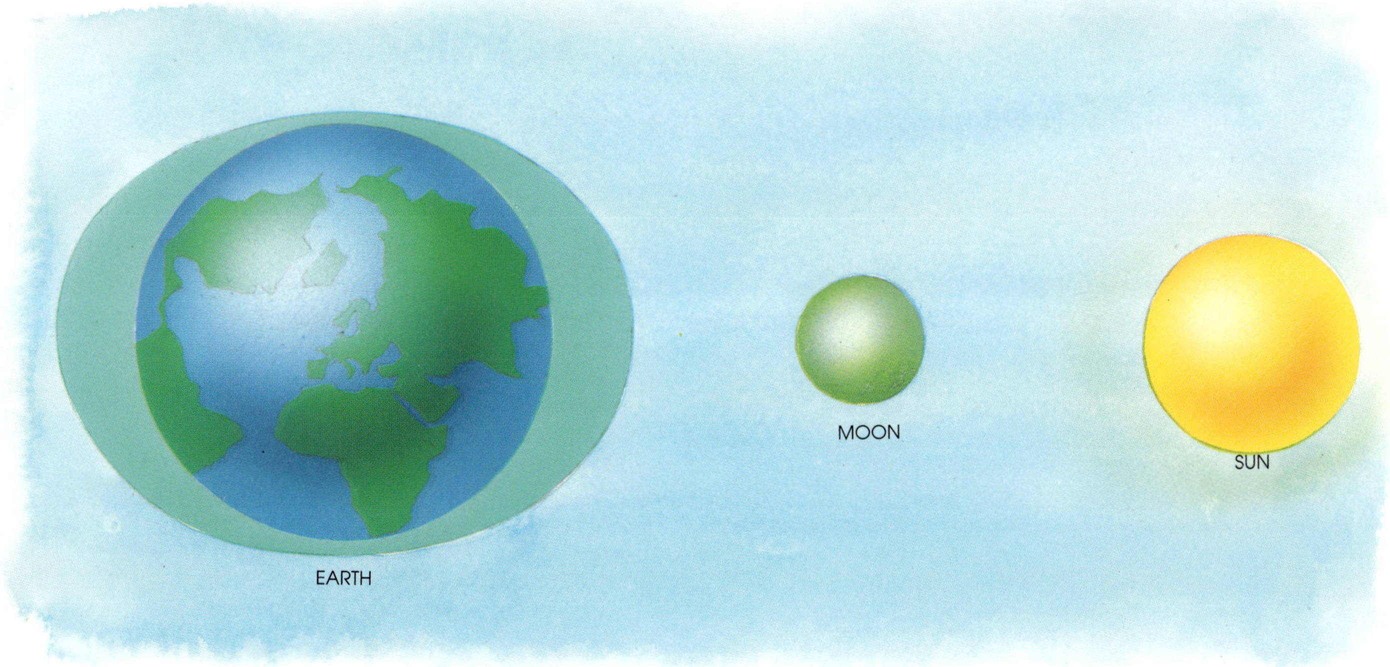

Raising a family

All animals and plants must reproduce to ensure that their species does not become extinct. The sea can be a rather dangerous place for a small, helpless creature to live, so in many species the parents try to improve their young's chances of survival.

SEAHORSE

Why is the seahorse so special?

It is the male seahorse that gives birth to the young! The male has a pouch, rather like that of a kangaroo, which becomes swollen at the start of the breeding season. Using a long egg-laying tube, the female lays up to 200 eggs in her mate's pouch. After about six weeks the tiny seahorses are ready to hatch from the eggs in the father's pouch. The male seahorse grips a piece of seaweed with his tail and wriggles and squirms to push the babies out of the pouch. It may take him as long as two days to give birth to all the babies, after which he is absolutely exhausted.

What is a 'mermaid's purse'?

Just as a bird lays an egg, some female sharks and rays produce an eggcase called a 'mermaid's purse'. The female dogshark, for example, lays her eggs in these cases and attaches them by means of long tendrils to seaweed or soft coral. Inside the egg case there is also a large yolk, which serves as food for the growing shark. After six to nine months the young shark is large enough to break out of the case and swim weakly away.

MERMAID'S PURSE

Which little zooplankton can reproduce without mating?

The water flea. The female deposits her eggs in a brood pouch, where they all develop into identical females that are miniature versions of their mother. Some of these 'daughters' already have eggs developing inside them – even before they are big enough to be released from their mother's pouch! This means that the mother can be carrying her own granddaughters! When conditions in the sea become harsh, with cold temperatures and a shortage of food, the water flea suddenly starts producing eggs that develop into males. The males and females then mate and produce young that are better able to survive the harsh conditions.

WATER FLEA

When are shrimps, crabs and crayfish 'in berry'?

When they are carrying their eggs, which look like little berries. After they have been fertilized by the male, the female lays the eggs and cements them to structures on the underside of her tail segments, called pleopods. In this way she increases their chances of surviving until they are ready to hatch. The young then float away to begin life on their own, although many still die before they reach adulthood.

CRAYFISH

CARDINALFISH

Which fish keeps its eggs in its mouth?

The cardinalfish. After the female cardinalfish lays her eggs, the male fertilizes them and then gently sucks them up into his mouth, where he incubates them until they are ready to hatch. The fish probably do this to keep the eggs safe from predators and from being swept away in the currents. Fish that have this strange behaviour are called mouthbrooders.

How do giant clams manage to mate?

Giant clams can weigh hundreds of kilograms, and are fixed in one place. Because they cannot move around to find mates, these clams reproduce by releasing their eggs and sperm, or spawn, at the same time. The spawn released by the first giant clam triggers others to release their's too. Because the spawn can get swept away by the currents, or be eaten by fish, the giant clams each produce massive amounts of spawn to make up for any that may be lost.

GIANT CLAM

Growing up

Sometimes young animals are very different from their parents, in both appearance and behaviour. This is certainly very true of many of the creatures which live in the sea and on the shore. They have an advantage in that they don't need to compete with their parents for food or a home.

HERMIT CRAB

Which crab goes house-hunting?

The hermit crab. This crab always lives in the empty shells of other animals, and as it grows it needs to move into larger and larger homes. When it sees an empty shell it feels about inside it with its nippers, to check that it is large enough and that no other animal is living there. Once the shell passes this first test the hermit crab quickly swops shells to try the new one out for fit and weight. If the shell is not suitable the crab returns to the old one before another hermit crab can steal it.

Do some periwinkles migrate as they grow?

Yes. The periwinkle *Littorina* starts life high on the shore so that it is not washed off the rocks by waves. But as the periwinkle grows it becomes strong enough to resist the waves, and so it moves down the shore and closer to the sea where there is more food to eat.

PERIWINKLES

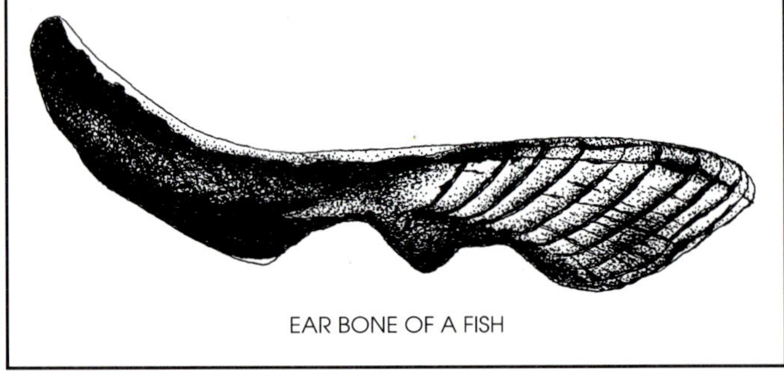

EAR BONE OF A FISH

How can scientists tell the age of a fish?

By studying its ear bones! These little bones, called otoliths, have rings of growth, rather like those of a tree trunk. Normally, two rings are laid down each year, so by counting the number of rings, scientists can work out the age of the fish. Once they know this they can compare it to the length of the fish's body, and then work out how fast the fish grows. This is useful because it reveals when the fish will reach maturity and start producing eggs.

Do some fish have a sex change?

Yes. One example is the cleaner wrasse, which lives in small groups. Each group consists of a male and his harem of females. The male is the oldest fish in the group, and if he dies the oldest female begins to act like a male, controlling the other females in the group and also patrolling the borders of the territory. After about two weeks the fish has undergone a complete sex change, and is able to mate with females in the harem.

CLEANER WRASSE

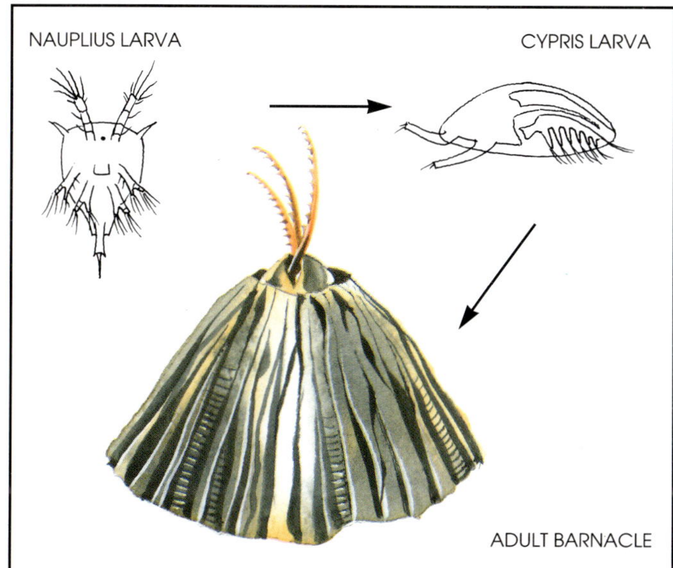

Does the barnacle stand on its head?

Yes, but only when it is ready to change into an adult. A barnacle starts life as a little swimming animal, called a nauplius larva, but as it grows it moults six times before turning into a cypris larva, which is enclosed in a shell with two halves. It is now ready to change into an adult barnacle, but first it must find a place to settle. It feels around with its antennae, testing that there is enough space on the rock and that it receives enough light and water current. The larva then stands on its head and glues itself onto the rock with cement made in a gland in the antennae. It twists itself around so that the legs it once used for swimming are now kicked out into the water and used for filter-feeding. Within a few days the barnacle has become a fully formed adult, protected inside a cone-shaped shell that can be closed with a 'door' at low tide.

Why does the emperor angelfish change colour?

Like many other fishes, the emperor angelfish changes colour as it grows up. When it is young it is dark blue with white and light blue rings. This colour pattern camouflages the fish by breaking up its outline in the silvery blue water so that it confuses its predators. The adult is more colourful, with bright yellow stripes on a brown background. This is because it now has its own territory, and uses its colours to warn others not to trespass. But this bright colour pattern also makes the adult fish very obvious to predators, so it has a dark stripe hiding its vulnerable eyes.

EMPEROR ANGELFISH

Moving around

Most animals must be able to move around to search for food and mates, and to escape from their enemies. We all know that fish can swim, but other creatures that live in the sea or on the seashore use some very interesting methods to move around.

FLYING FISH

Do flying fish really fly?

No, because they cannot flap their fins. But if they are being chased they leap out of the water and spread their wide fins so that they glide for up to 100 metres before they fall back into the sea. Most predators are so confused when the flying fish disappear from the sea by leaping into the air that they give up the chase.

How do squid swim so fast?

By jet propulsion! Water is drawn into the muscular mantle cavity and then forced out through a funnel. This jet of water propels the squid backwards, and because the funnel can be pointed in any direction, the squid can quickly change course if it is being chased or is trying to catch a darting fish.

SCALLOPS

Which creatures swim by clapping through the water?

Scallops. These animals are bivalves, which means that they have a shell of two halves joined by a hinge, like a mussel or a clam. They lie on their side on the sea bed and, if they are threatened, can quickly escape by clapping the two halves of the shell together. In this way, water is drawn into the shell and then quickly forced out in a jet, which propels the scallop backwards through the water.

Are any sea creatures surfers?

Yes, the plough shell, *Bullia*. It is a scavenger which feeds on dead and dying animals washed up on the beach, such as blue-bottles and jellyfish. At low tide it remains buried in the sand, with only its tubular siphon sticking out. As the tide rises, the plough shell emerges from the sand and uses its wide foot to help it surf ashore. Once on the beach, it can quickly detect its prey with its powerful sense of smell. After it has eaten its fill, the plough shell buries itself in the sand again and waits until the tide turns before it emerges and surfs back to its low tide position, so that it does not get stranded on the hot, dry beach.

Can mudskippers walk on land?

Yes – even though they have no legs! Mudskippers are small fish that live in tropical estuaries and mangrove swamps. They use their strong, muscular fins to skip across the mud from pool to pool. Before leaving each pool they swallow a mouthful of water which they store in their gill chambers. They can then breathe while on land by taking oxygen from this water.

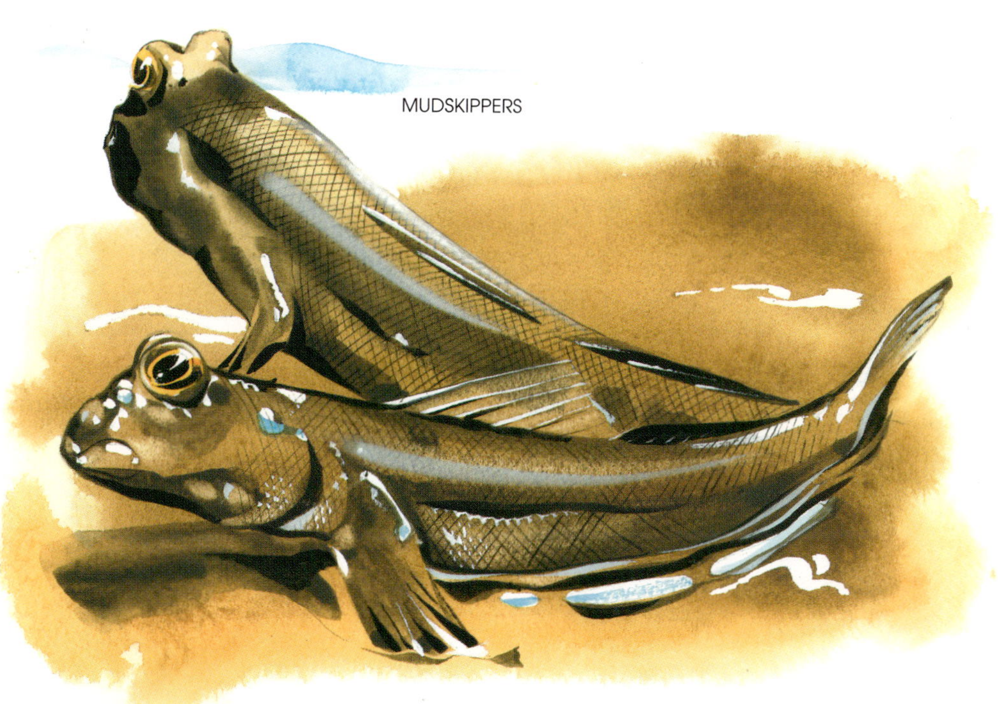

Why do crabs run sideways?

To stop them from tripping over their own feet! Crabs have five pairs of legs, set quite closely together, and if they tried to move forwards quickly each leg would become tangled up with the one in front of it.

GHOST CRAB

Are there ghosts on our beaches?

No, but there are ghost crabs on beaches along our east coast. Ghost crabs can run at lightning speed. They only emerge from their burrows at dusk to scavenge for food cast up on the beach. Because the crabs are a rather pale colour which camouflages them against the sand, sometimes only their shadows can be seen in the moonlight as they dart in and out of their burrows and run across the sand, giving them a ghost-like appearance.

The drifters

BLUE-BOTTLE

Some animals save their energy by drifting along on the sea's surface, rather than trying to swim against the currents. Because these animals have no way of escaping predators, most of them are coloured blue so that they are well camouflaged in the sea.

Why is a blue-bottle like an iceberg?

Because, like an iceberg, most of it is below the surface of the water, and what we see is only a small part of the whole body. The blue-bottle is actually a colony of small creatures, each with their own special function. The part that we see floating on the waves is simply called the float. It is pumped up with nitrogen and carbon monoxide gas from a small gas gland on its side. Every few minutes the float flops sideways into the water to prevent it from drying out. Below the float hang long fishing tentacles, bearing stinging cells which paralyse prey such as small fish. The tentacles can contract so that they can pass the prey to the feeding individuals of the colony. The other members of the blue-bottle colony produce young blue-bottles, which remain attached to the adult until they are large enough to break free and drift away.

What is a by-the-wind sailor?

A little animal whose proper name is *Velella*. It is a relative of the blue-bottle, but has a flat, oval float and a sail which allows it to be blown across the surface of the sea like a windsurfer. The *Velella*'s stinging tentacles allow it to catch small creatures swimming just below the surface of the water.

Who gulps air to stay afloat?

The floating sea slug, *Glaucus*. The bubble of air in its stomach keeps it afloat while it drifts across the sea surface in search of its favourite food, the blue-bottles. It can even use the stinging cells of the blue-bottles in its own tissues to defend itself from predators! The stinging cells of blue-bottles have little darts that shoot out and inject poison into prey or predators. But when *Glaucus* swallows them, the darts do not fire. Instead they pass through the wall of the gut and into the skin of the sea slug, ready to sting any attacker.

GLAUCUS

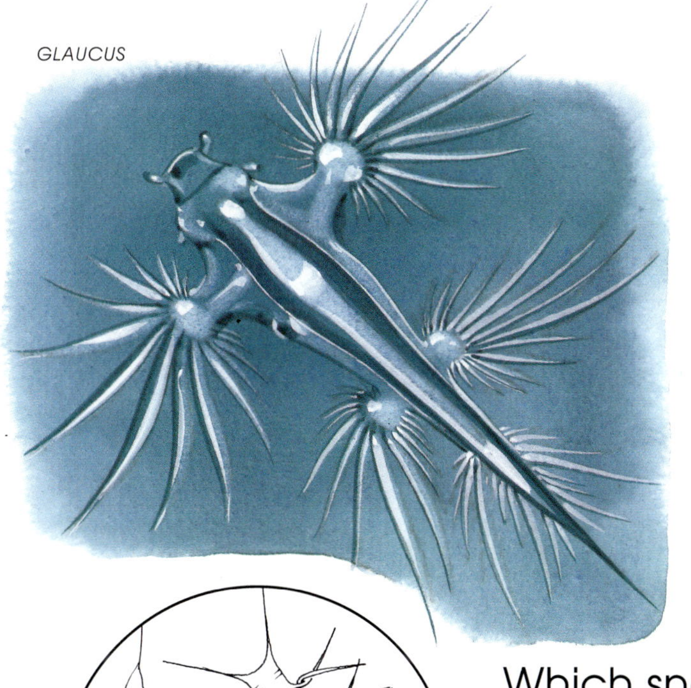

GOOSE BARNACLES

How do goose barnacles travel the world?

They get a ride on any floating object on which they can settle, using it as a raft. They are attached to the raft by means of a long, fleshy stalk, and they scoop plankton, such as diatoms, from the water using feeding structures called cirri. Some types of goose barnacle attach themselves to whales and are specially adapted so that the current created by the moving whale flows right through the barnacles, without them having to stick out their cirri. Scientists use the patterns of these barnacles to identify individual whales, allowing them to keep track of the whales' movements and to study their behaviour.

DIATOMS

Which snail blows a raft of bubbles?

The bubble-raft shell, called *Janthina*. This pretty blue snail secretes a foam of bubbles that floats on the surface of the sea. The snail hangs upside down from this floating raft and drifts about the sea, feeding on blue-bottles and their relatives.

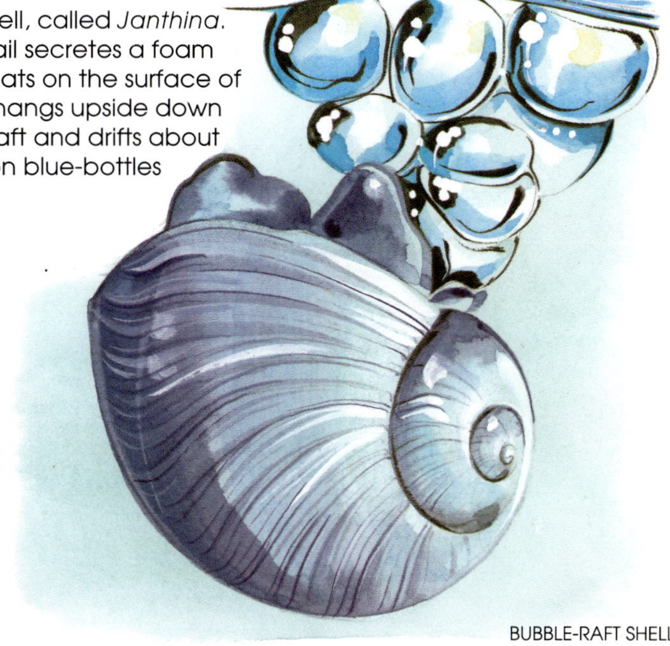

BUBBLE-RAFT SHELL

Why do diatoms have such spiky shapes?

So that they do not sink to the bottom of the sea too quickly. Diatoms are a kind of phytoplankton, the microscopic plants in the sea, which many sea creatures rely on for food. Like all plants they need light to survive and grow, so they must stay near the surface of the sea. They cannot swim, so to prevent them from sinking to the deeper, darker reaches of the ocean, they have spiky shapes which are caught by tiny currents and keep the diatoms tumbling about near the sea's surface.

Finding the way

The sea is a huge place in which to live, with no street signs or maps to show the way. Also, sandy beaches and rocky shores must appear never-ending to the tiny creatures that live there. How do these animals find their way?

BEACHED PILOT WHALES

Do dolphins and whales sometimes get lost?

Yes. For some reason that is not yet understood, there are often mass strandings of dolphins or whales on shores around the world. Even if the animals are helped out to sea, many of them swim straight back to the shore again. Unfortunately many of these animals die each year.

Do young lobsters tour the ocean before settling down?

Yes. When spiny lobsters hatch they are caught up in a massive current called the south Atlantic gyre, which carries them in a huge circle between Africa and South America. Somehow they realize when they are back in their home waters again, and only then do they change into their adult form, swim out of the current and settle to the sea bed.

Do limpets leave trails to help them return home?

Yes. As limpets grow, their shells mould and seal perfectly around small depressions and bumps in the rocks. Each day the limpets set off to feed on algae which they scrape off the rocks. They lay down slimy trails of mucus as they go to help them glide along. Once they have eaten their fill, they return home by retracing their way along their own mucus trail, and then snuggle down into exactly the same position. The limpets may also be able to recognize tiny landmarks such as bumps and scrapes in the rock surface.

LIMPETS

ROCK LOBSTER

SAND HOPPERS

How do turtle hatchlings find the sea?

For many years, scientists believed that the hatchlings were attracted to the brightness of the moon shining over the sea and the sparkling waves. However, the hatchlings can also find their way on quite dark, moonless nights. It is now thought that they crawl away from the dark outlines of the sand dunes and beach vegetation, setting a course which will naturally lead them to the waves. At some turtle nesting sites in America, all the lights near the beach are switched off during the hatching season, so that the young turtles don't get confused and head in the wrong direction.

Who uses the sun as a compass?

The sand hoppers, which swarm over their favourite food of rotting kelp on the beach. They emerge from the sand at sunset, but wait until the moon rises before they hop down the beach to feed. At dawn they return to the high tide mark to bury themselves in the sand. They orientate themselves in relation to the sun's position at dusk and dawn. If the sand hoppers are moved to another beach, they lose their way and move in the wrong direction. This means that their navigating ability must be inherited from their parents and is suited only to the beach on which they were born.

RAY

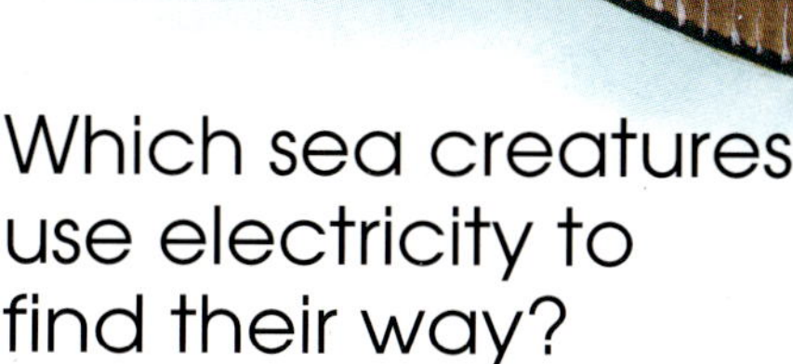

Which sea creatures use electricity to find their way?

Sharks and rays. Small structures on their heads, called the ampullae of Lorenzini, can detect weak electric fields. These allow sharks and rays to orientate themselves in relation to the Earth's electric fields. They can also detect the weak electric field generated by the activity of muscles and nerves of their prey. Recently, scientists at the Natal Sharks Board have developed a new type of shark barrier by using electricity to turn sharks away from beaches.

SHARK

Camouflage

STONEFISH

Animals camouflage themselves to avoid attack by predators and to hide themselves while they lie in ambush for prey. They do this by either blending with their surroundings or by disguising themselves to look like other plants and animals that are ignored by predators.

What is a stonefish?

A fish that disguises itself as a stone on the sea floor. It has a rough, warty skin, and it keeps so still that it blends in perfectly with the stones around it. For this reason, someone walking in shallow water on the beach may step on it accidentally. When this happens the stonefish defends itself by injecting poison from spines along its back into the person's foot.

SPONGE CRAB

Can sand shrimps change their colour?

Yes. When these shrimps are swimming in clear water or sitting on a light background, such as sand, they are see-through except for some dark stripes which help to break up their outline. But when they sit on a dark background, such as a rock, they become a dark brown. They are able to camouflage themselves by changing colour because they have small pigment cells in the skin, which can contract to let the background colour show through or expand to darken the shrimp.

SAND SHRIMP

Which crab hides under a sponge?

The sponge crab. It cuts out a piece of sponge with its claws and holds it over its back with its last pair of legs, which are specially adapted for this purpose. After a while the sponge grows so that it fits around the crab. Predators mistake the crab for a sponge, which is unpleasant to eat, so they ignore the crab and look elsewhere for a meal.

COWRIES

How do cowries hide their shells?

By disguising them with a cloak of skin. Although cowries are famous for their beautiful shells, their shells are often covered by a fleshy layer of skin called the mantle. The blotchy colours and irregular bumps on the mantle make it look just like a piece of seaweed or allows it to blend in with the sponges on which most cowries feed. If this camouflage does not fool an alert predator, the cowrie can still protect itself by withdrawing into its shell.

Why do some fish have dark backs and pale bellies?

To make them invisible to predators. This special colour pattern is called countershading, and is common in fish which live near the sea surface. Seen from above by a predator such as a seabird, the fish blends in with the dark water below, and seen from below, the pale belly matches the silvery sunlight at the sea surface.

FLATFISH

COUNTERSHADING

Which fishes have twisted faces?

The flatfishes. When they start life, they look like normal fish and swim near the sea surface, but after a few weeks one eye has gradually moved round so that both eyes are on the same side of the head, and the front of the head has twisted. This is because the fish spends the rest of its life lying flat on its side on the sea floor, perfectly camouflaged from predators and prey. Sometimes it partly buries itself under the sand, with only its eyes sticking out, but its colours also help it to blend in with its surroundings. The upper side of the fish is a mottled brown colour, while the underside, which is hidden from view and so does not need to be camouflaged, is a plain pale colour. The flatfishes can even change colour to match the sand they are lying on. Like the sand shrimp, small pigment cells in the skin can contract to let the background colour show through, or expand to make the fish a darker colour.

Self-defence

Not all animals rely on camouflage to defend themselves from predators – some have developed dangerous weapons or strange behaviour patterns to either fight off attack or help them escape.

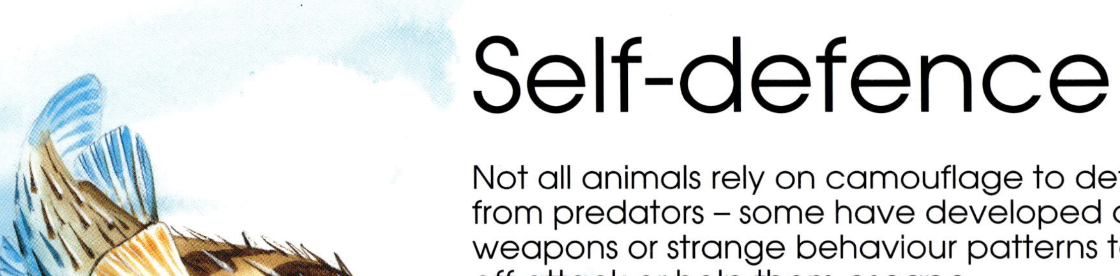

PORCUPINE FISH

Which fish is like a porcupine?

The porcupine fish, which defends itself by being prickly, just like a porcupine. When relaxed it looks much like any other fish, because the spines lie flat against the body. But if the fish is threatened it inflates itself with water, or air if it is caught and pulled out of the water, so that the spines stick out. The porcupine fish is too prickly to attack, and is now too large for most predators to swallow.

Do sea cucumbers vomit on their enemies?

No, but it sometimes looks as if they do. If they are threatened by a predator they may expel part or all of the gut. This distracts the surprised predator, and while it gobbles up the gut, the sea cucumber can escape. Luckily, the sea cucumber can grow a new gut. Some sea cucumbers cannot do this, so they entangle their attacker with a mass of sticky threads shot out from the hind end. While the attacker struggles to free itself, the sea cucumber has time to crawl away.

SEA CUCUMBER

Do mussels sometimes tie down their attackers?

Yes. Mussels are preyed upon by whelks, which drill a hole through the mussels' shells so that they can feed on the tissues inside. They do this with their rasping 'tongue', or radula, and acid which helps soften the shell. But the mussels can sometimes defend themselves by tying down the whelks with their byssus threads, which are usually used for attaching the mussels to the rocks.

How does the brittle star escape from its enemies?

By breaking off its own arm! Its five arms are much thinner than those of its relatives, the starfish, and as the name suggests, are very brittle. If a predator grabs hold of one of the arms, the brittle star breaks off the arm so that it can escape. The brittle star then immediately starts to grow a new arm in its place.

BRITTLE STAR

Which crab boxes its attackers?

The boxer crab. It carries a small anemone in each of its nippers, and if it is attacked it thrusts out one nipper after the other, like a sparring boxer. In this way it tries to sting the attacker with the anemone and make it give up the fight.

FIREFISH

Does the firefish defend itself with fire?

No, but its wavy fins look like flames, and the spines in the fins can inject a poison that causes a burning pain. Although it is related to the ugly stonefish, which camouflages itself with drab colours, the firefish uses its bright colours to warn predators that it is poisonous.

Finding food

Like all other plants, seaweeds and phytoplankton, the microscopic plants found in the sea, use sunlight to make their own food from simple chemicals in their environment. But animals cannot do this, and must eat plants or other animals to survive.

How did the mantis shrimp get its name?

It looks rather like a praying mantis insect, because it has a strong pair of special legs folded beneath its body as if it were praying, and well-developed, stalked eyes. Most mantis shrimps wait at the entrance of their burrows for passing prey, such as shrimp and fish, which they spear with spines on the special legs. Others stalk their prey and use the powerful legs to smash the shells of clams and crabs, which they then carry back to the burrow to eat.

Which snails shoot their prey with a poison arrow?

The cone shells. The teeth of these pretty sea snails have become modified into hundreds of tiny arrows which they store in a sac inside their body. When they find prey, such as a worm or a fish, they shoot stab or one of these arrows into the prey. Poison carried within the hollow arrow paralyses the prey and, because the snail is then in no danger of being injured in a fight, it can swallow prey almost as big as itself!

PARROTFISH

Which fish crunches coral?

The parrotfish. It gets its name because it is so colourful and has strong teeth which are all fused together to look like a parrot's beak. It uses these teeth to bite off chunks of coral and chew them up so that it can feed on the soft coral polyps and on small algae that live in the tissues of the coral.

Do perlemoen trap their food?

Yes. Young perlemoen feed by scraping tiny plants, or algae, off the rocks with a toothed 'tongue' called a radula. But as they get older they trap drifting pieces of kelp by raising the front of the shell and then clamping down tightly over the kelp. During stormy weather, when strong currents sweep through the kelp bed, the perlemoen may also clamp down on the tip of a swaying frond of kelp. Sometimes a number of perlemoen work together to trap a large frond of kelp, which is then shared by them all.

SPINY STARFISH

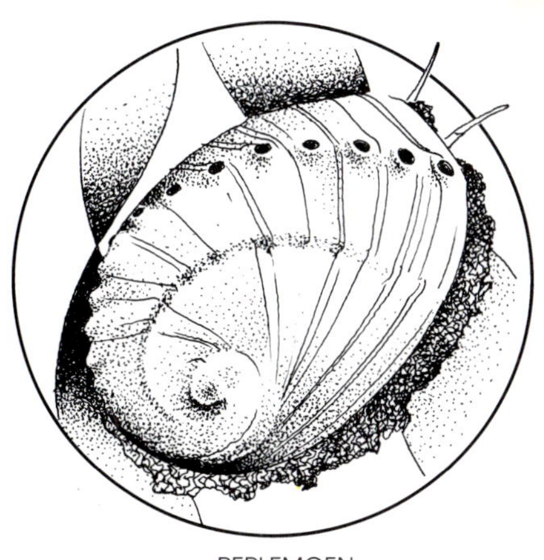

PERLEMOEN

Can a starfish eat through its stomach?

Yes. The favourite food of the spiny starfish are mussels, which protect themselves from most predators by clamping together the two halves of their shell. But this large starfish has hundreds of tube feet on the underside of each of its five arms, which can exert a powerful grip. They can prise open a mussel shell until there is enough space for the starfish to push its stomach into the gap and release digestive juices that break down the mussel's flesh. The food can then be sucked up into the starfish's gut.

Why is a goatfish like a billy goat?

It has two long fleshy whiskers, called barbels, hanging down from the chin. The goatfish wiggles the barbels, which are equipped with special taste organs, in the sand to search for prey such as worms, shrimps and small fish. If the barbels disturb prey the goatfish snatches them up into its mouth. Other fish often follow closely behind to eat any prey that the goatfish misses.

Do dolphins zap their prey with sonar?

Yes. Sonar is a method of location using echoes. By bouncing sounds off a target and analysing how quickly they echo back, dolphins can locate schools of fish. They can fine-tune this echolocation by producing about 500 click sounds every second as they get closer to their unsuspecting prey. It is also thought that dolphins can stun fish with these high-pitched clicks so that they are easier to catch. During a feeding frenzy a dolphin can switch the sonar off instantly if another dolphin swims in front of it, so that it does not hurt its companions.

GOATFISH

Filter feeders

Many animals in the sea do not move about to search for food, but wait for tiny particles of food to float to them. They then use special filters to sift the food from the water. These filter-feeders either eat the ocean's microscopic plant life (phytoplankton), tiny animals (zooplankton), or pieces of dead and rotting plant and animal material, called detritus.

Which mussel feeds through a straw?

The white mussel. It digs into the sand until it is hidden below the surface, and extends two siphons into the water. The shorter of the two, called the inhalent siphon, is like a straw because it sucks in water. Phytoplankton and detritus in the water are trapped by the mussel's gills, and the water is then forced out through the longer, exhalent siphon. The inhalent siphon has a sieve across its opening to prevent sand from clogging up the gills.

How do paddles help the mud prawn feed?

They help it filter food from the water. The mud prawn wedges itself into its U-shaped burrow and uses the paddle-like pleopods under its tail to force a current of water through the burrow. Plankton and detritus are filtered out of this water by fringed hairs on the prawn's mouthparts and its first pair of legs.

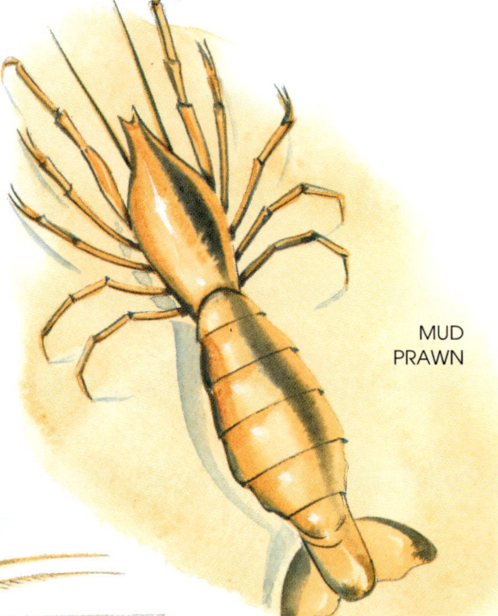

Did you know?

Sometimes mussels are killed when they filter-feed large amounts of poisonous phytoplankton during a red tide. Red tides are caused when some phytoplankton, called dinoflagellates, multiply rapidly or 'bloom' during certain ideal conditions. Poisonous dinoflagellates can paralyse white mussels, which are then washed up on beaches. If these mussels are eaten, they can paralyse or even kill a person. But most red tides are caused by dinoflagellates which are not poisonous, although they can still kill mussels by clogging their gills.

MOLE CRAB

Which crab filter-feeds with its antennae?

The mole crab. This strange-looking crab lives in the surf zone on beaches in Natal, and migrates up and down the beach with the waves as the tide rises and falls. It uses its spade-like legs to dig backwards into the sand, until only its stalked eyes and two pairs of antennae are visible. These antennae, which are fringed with hairs, are held out to filter food particles from the water.

What is a feather duster worm?

A filter-feeding worm which looks like a feather duster. It is also called a fan worm, because its feathery filaments are in the shape of a fan and are all you can usually see of the worm. The rest of the body is protected inside a tube which the worm builds from sand grains mixed with mucus. Particles in the water are trapped on the filaments, which are covered with tiny hairs that sweep the particles into a groove leading to the mouth. This groove sorts the food – small particles are carried straight to the mouth, while medium-sized particles are stored in a pair of sacs near the mouth until they can be used to fix the tube. Large particles cannot fit into the groove, so are rejected.

Why do sea squirts sometimes squirt?

To spit out water after they have filtered out their food. These creatures are sometimes seen squirting water quite high into the air at low tide. The most familiar sea squirt is the large red-bait, *Pyura*, which is often used by fishermen as bait, but some sea squirts are small and transparent, and live in colonies. Sea squirts feed by sucking up water through an inhalent siphon into the pharynx, a sieve-like structure dotted with holes. As the water flows out through the holes, food particles are trapped in a sticky mucus and are then swept into the sea squirts' stomach. The filtered water is then squirted out through an exhalent siphon.

Which are the largest filter feeders?

Baleen whales. These whales do not have teeth, but comb-like structures called baleen plates which hang from their upper jaw. Most of these whales feed on krill, a shrimp-like zooplankton which in turn feeds on phytoplankton. After taking a mouthful of seawater, the whale uses its tongue to force the water out through the baleen plates so that the krill are trapped against them. The blue whale, which is the largest animal in the world, eats about four tons of krill every day!

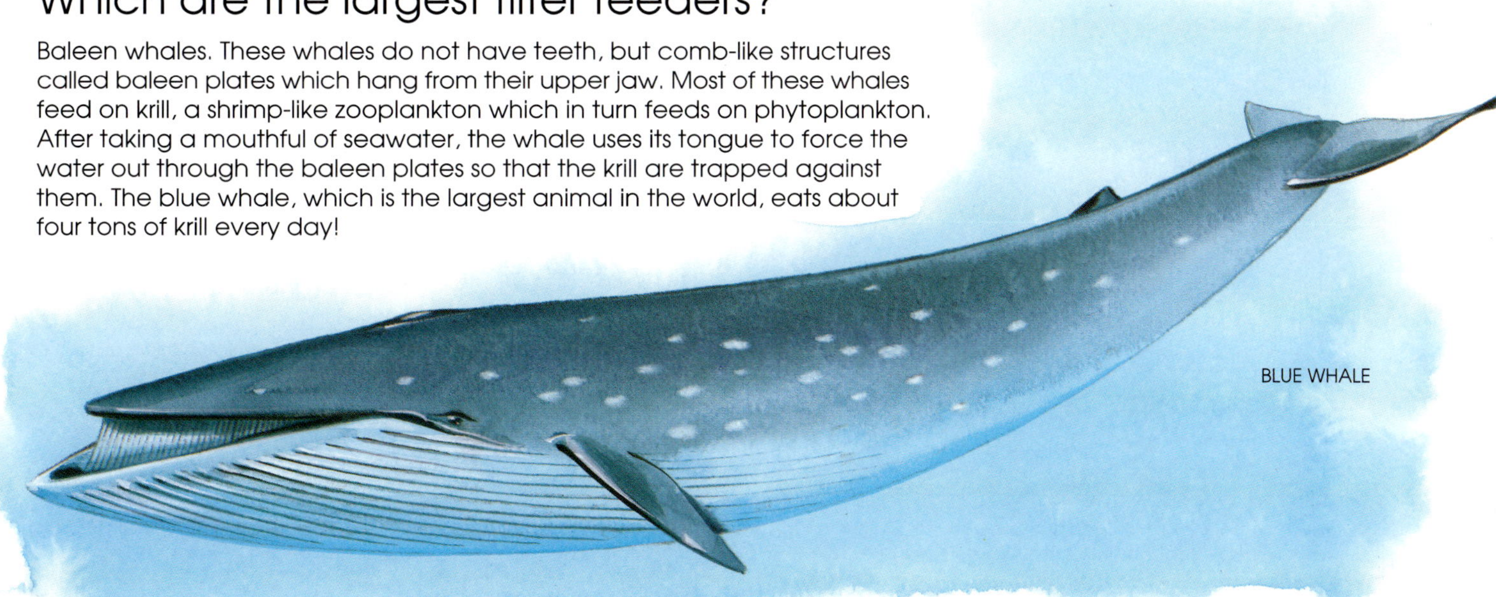

Communication

SEALS

Animals need to pass information on to each other for many different reasons. They may want to scare other animals off their territories, attract and impress a mate, or warn others about approaching danger, but they all have a unique way of communicating with each other.

How does a mother seal find her pup?

She calls the pup to her. About a week after giving birth the mother seal has to leave her pup for a while so that she can return to the sea to feed. While she is away her pup moves around playing with other 'orphans'. When she returns, she has to find her pup amongst thousands of identical-looking pups, so she moves through the colony, calling loudly as she goes. Several pups may run towards her, all hoping that it is their mother that has returned, but she sniffs each one until she recognizes the smell of her own pup.

Can dolphins and whales 'talk'?

Yes, they have their own 'languages'. Whales communicate with squeaks and moans that can travel long distances through the water to call males and females together during the breeding season. Dolphins communicate with high-pitched clicks and whistles. Although these sounds don't travel as far as the whales' songs, they are an important form of communication for dolphins. When they are swimming in a school, they use clicks to send messages to each other, but as they get more excited during feeding frenzies or encounters with other dolphin schools they whistle constantly.

BOTTLE-NOSED DOLPHINS

How do pistol shrimps warn off intruders?

These shrimps have one nipper that is much larger than the other, and which they can snap closed to make a popping sound, rather like when we snap our fingers. Pistol shrimps control a territory around their burrows, and if another pistol shrimp crosses the borders of the territory, the loud snap from the nipper warns the unwelcome intruder that it is trespassing.

Do fiddler crabs wave at their mates?

Yes. Although female fiddler crabs have two equal-sized claws, males have one claw which is much bigger than the other and which becomes brightly coloured during the breeding season. The male waves this claw up and down to attract the attention of a female, and to lure her into his burrow so that they can mate. Several different species of fiddler crabs may live on the same beach, but they must only mate with crabs of their own species. Each species therefore has its own distinctive way of waving, so that females can recognize males of their species.

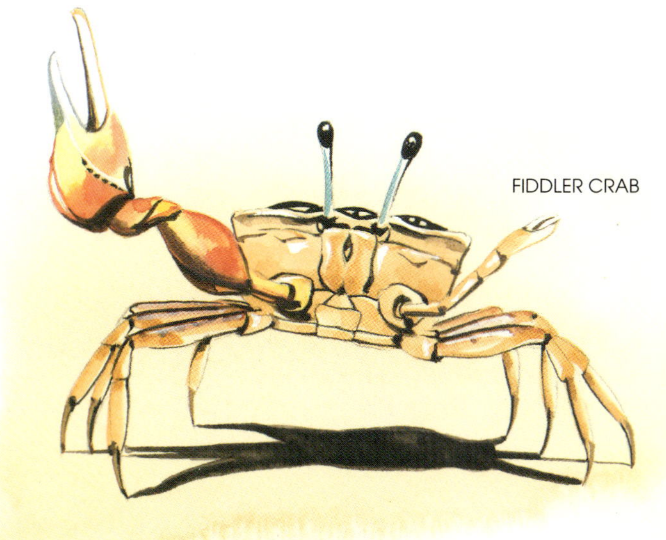

Can an octopus flush with excitement?

Yes. If it sees prey, such as a crab, it gets so excited that it flushes a darker colour. A male octopus may also use this colour-changing ability to impress a female during courtship. However, if the octopus is scared by an animal larger than itself, it pales in fear. It flattens its body and turns almost white except for dark patches round its eyes. This makes the octopus seem larger than it actually is, which might frighten away the attacker. The octopus is able to communicate with colour in this way because it has small pigment cells in its skin, which are stretched or contracted by tiny muscles.

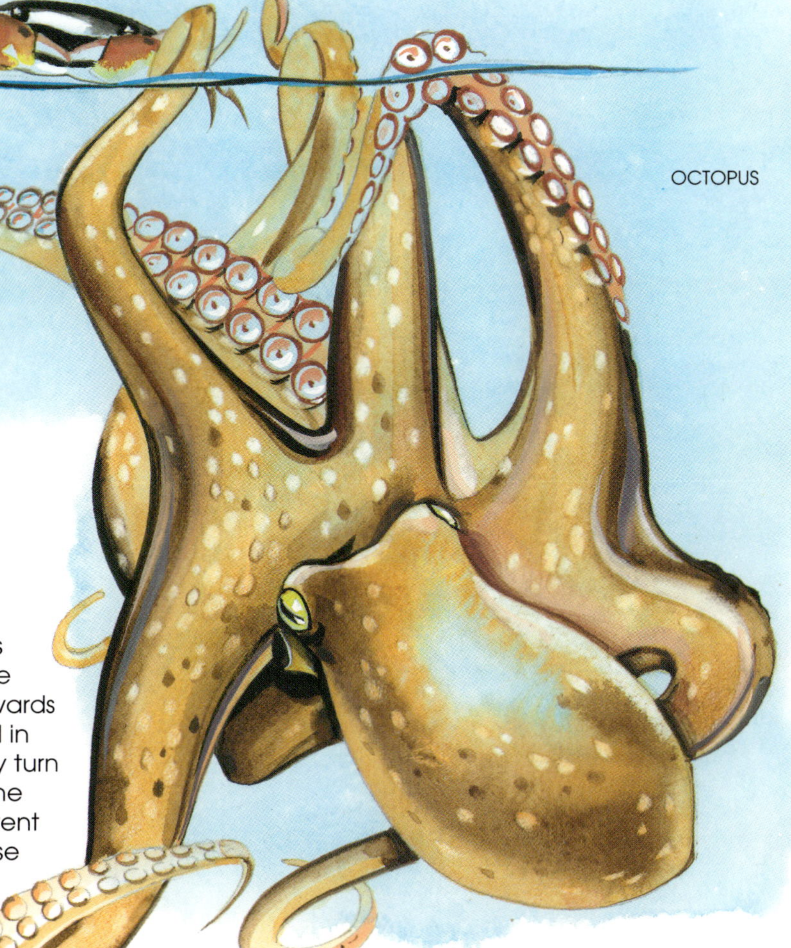

Why do cowfish dance together?

It is part of their courtship display. When the male cowfish is ready to mate he swims into the female's territory and rocks back and forth in front of her. The female then leads him in a slow, spiral dance up towards the surface of the sea to show that she is interested in him too. When they are just below the surface, they turn tail to tail and the female releases her eggs while the male releases his sperm. They then swim off in different directions. These fish are named after cows because they have little horns on the front of their heads.

Living together

Many organisms in the sea live together in close relationships that often last their entire lives. In some of these relationships, both partners benefit by helping each other. This is called mutualism. In others, one partner benefits while the other is not affected in any way, and this is called commensalism.

Do spiny lobsters have a bodyguard?

Yes. On the east coast spiny lobsters, which are the favourite food of octopuses, often share their shelters with a moray eel. If an octopus tries to pull a lobster from its shelter, the moray eel attacks the octopus and eats it! Both animals benefit from this relationship because, while the lobster has its own bodyguard, the moray eel just has to wait for its meal to come along. Some lobsters don't have their own bodyguards, but if they are attacked they make a shrill noise by rubbing the bases of their antennae against a ridge on their hard shell. When the moray eel hears this alarm call, it goes rushing to the rescue.

Does the blind shrimp have a housemate?

Yes. Some types of gobies, which are small fish, share a burrow in the sandy sea bed with the blind shrimp. The goby stands guard at the entrance to the burrow while the shrimp cleans and repairs their home. The shrimp only comes out to dump a pile of rubble when a flick from the goby's tail tells it that it is safe to do so. While it is outside the burrow, the shrimp keeps in contact with the goby with its long antennae. If danger threatens, the goby dives down the burrow, closely followed by its friend. In return for being a lookout for the shrimp, the goby has a safe place to live.

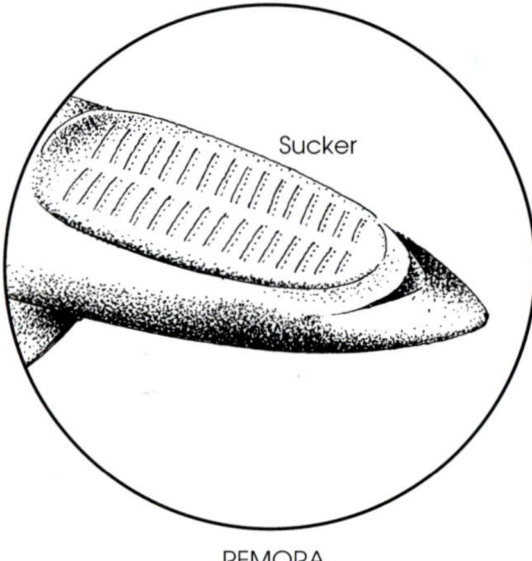

REMORA

Do some fish really hitch-hike?

Yes. The remora is a strange fish which has a large sucker on the top of its head with which it attaches itself to a shark. Not only does the remora get a free ride with the shark, and so does not waste its own energy by swimming, it also steals pieces of the shark's food! The shark does not seem to mind the remora, but it doesn't get anything in return for its generosity.

What is a clown fish?

A colourful fish that lives on large tropical sea anemones. Although other fish get stung by the stinging cells on the anemones' tentacles, the clown fish is quite safe. It is thought that something in the slimy mucus layer covering the fish prevents the stinging cells from firing their poison darts. The clown fish is protected from predators that are scared of getting stung by the anemone, and it pays for its keep by clearing bits of shell and sand from between the anemone's tentacles.

Which shrimp sets up a service station?

The cleaner shrimp. It attracts the attention of fish by waving its antennae at them, and then cleans wounds and picks parasites and dead tissue off the fishes' skin or even inside their mouth with its pincers. The fish are so grateful that they always avoid eating the cleaner shrimp, which they recognize by its bright colours. Sometimes when the cleaner shrimp is very busy, a number of fish can be seen waiting their turn for service.

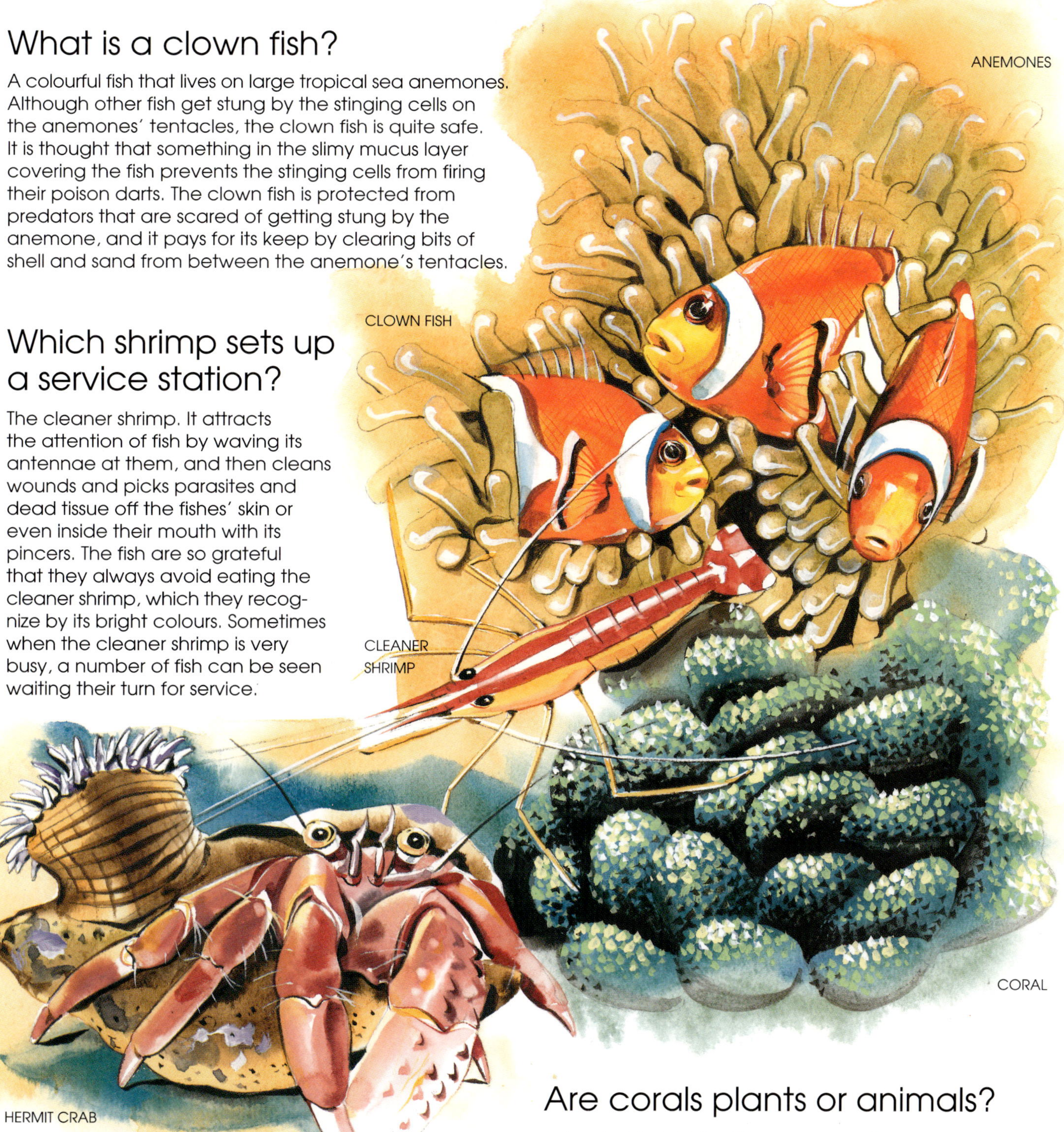

Why are some hermit crabs kidnappers?

They prise anemones off the rocks and transfer them to their own shells. In this way the hermit crabs are protected from predators by the stinging cells on the tentacles of the anemones. The anemones do not mind being kidnapped, because they are carried around to new areas which might have more food, and also share scraps of food caught by the hermit crab.

Are corals plants or animals?

Animals. At night the little anemone-like coral polyps stretch out their tentacles to prey on zooplankton, the tiny animal life floating in the sea. But during the day the polyps stay inside their 'skeleton', and rely on microscopic plant cells living within their tissues to provide them with food. Like all plants, these cells need light for photosynthesis, the process by which they make food. This is the reason why coral reefs are only found in clear, shallow waters, where there is enough light for the plant cells. In return for sharing their food with the coral, the plant cells have a place to live and use the waste products of the coral for photosynthesis.

Light in the sea

Like fireflies and glow-worms on land, some animals in the sea are luminescent, which means that they are able to produce light. They may use this special ability to defend themselves against predators, to find food, or even to attract a mate.

DEEP-SEA SQUID

How do some deep-sea squid escape predators?

They confuse them by squirting out a cloud of glowing ink. Other squid use black ink to surprise their enemies, but this would be useless to an animal that lives in the darkest depths of the ocean. Instead, these deep-sea squid rely on the luminescent cloud, which probably dazzles the predator as well as distracts it while the squid escapes.

Which fish uses light as bait?

The deep-sea anglerfish, which lives in the depths of the ocean. Because it is so dark down there, some fish are unable to hunt by sight. The anglerfish solves this problem in a very strange way. It has a luminous organ dangling from a 'fishing rod' held in front of its mouth, and when a curious animal such as a shrimp or small fish comes to investigate the light, it is snatched up by the powerful jaws of the anglerfish.

Why do waves sometimes sparkle at night?

Floating in the waves are large numbers of a dinoflagellate called *Noctiluca*, which means 'night light'. These are tiny, single-celled organisms which are only about one millimetre across. They are always present in the sea, but certain ideal conditions make them multiply very quickly, or bloom, so that millions bob about in the waves. As the waves break, tiny granules inside *Noctiluca* are stimulated to flash with light, so that the waves seem to sparkle at night.

DEEP-SEA ANGLERFISH

Why do hatchetfish have portholes of light?

So that their predators cannot see them from below. These fish live fairly deep in the ocean, where the light filtering down from the sea surface is dim. Light from the 'portholes' on the underside of the fish matches this dim light, ensuring that when seen from below the dark shape of the fish is not silhouetted against the light background of the sea surface above.

COMB JELLIES

Do comb jellies have fairy lights?

No, but it sometimes looks as if they do because they flicker with different colours. Comb jellies get their name from the rows of small hair-like structures called cilia, which 'comb' the water and propel the animal forwards. In the walls of the gut there are tiny granules that are luminescent, and because comb jellies are transparent, they light up the comb rows as they beat.

Why do krill flash when frightened?

To escape from their enemies. They have small light-producing organs, called photophores, on various parts of their body. If the krill is being chased, the bright flash stops the predator in its tracks, giving the krill time to escape. It also flashes each time it changes direction, so although the confused predator may snatch at the light, it cannot catch the darting krill.

What is a fish?

Fishes are cold-blooded, backboned animals that live in water. There are three different groups: jawless fishes; sharks and rays; and bony fishes. They are as different from one another as frogs, snakes, mammals and birds. The three different groups of fishes share a way of life in water and have many different forms.

How are fishes different from marine mammals?

A fish, such as a tuna or mullet, is a cold-blooded animal which breathes through its gills, normally has scales and fins, and either lays eggs or gives birth to live young. A marine mammal, such as a seal or otter, is warm-blooded, which means that it breathes air using its lungs, has a hairy or furry skin, and always gives birth to live young.

How many fins do fishes have?

A typical fish, such as a blacktail, has seven fins – two paired fins and three unpaired fins. The pectoral and pelvic fins are paired but the dorsal, tail and anal fins are unpaired and lie along the central line of the body. Many fishes have two dorsal fins. The dorsal, tail and anal fins of eels are joined.

Why do fishes have different body shapes?

Fishes have many different body shapes so that they can swim and feed in different ways. Oval, streamlined fishes, such as tunas, are designed to swim fast and to catch their prey at high speed. Flattened fishes, like skates, hunt along the bottom and hide themselves in the sand. Eels are long and thin so that they can feed and shelter in narrow crevices. Butterflyfishes are narrow so that they can squeeze through small gaps and dart to and fro.

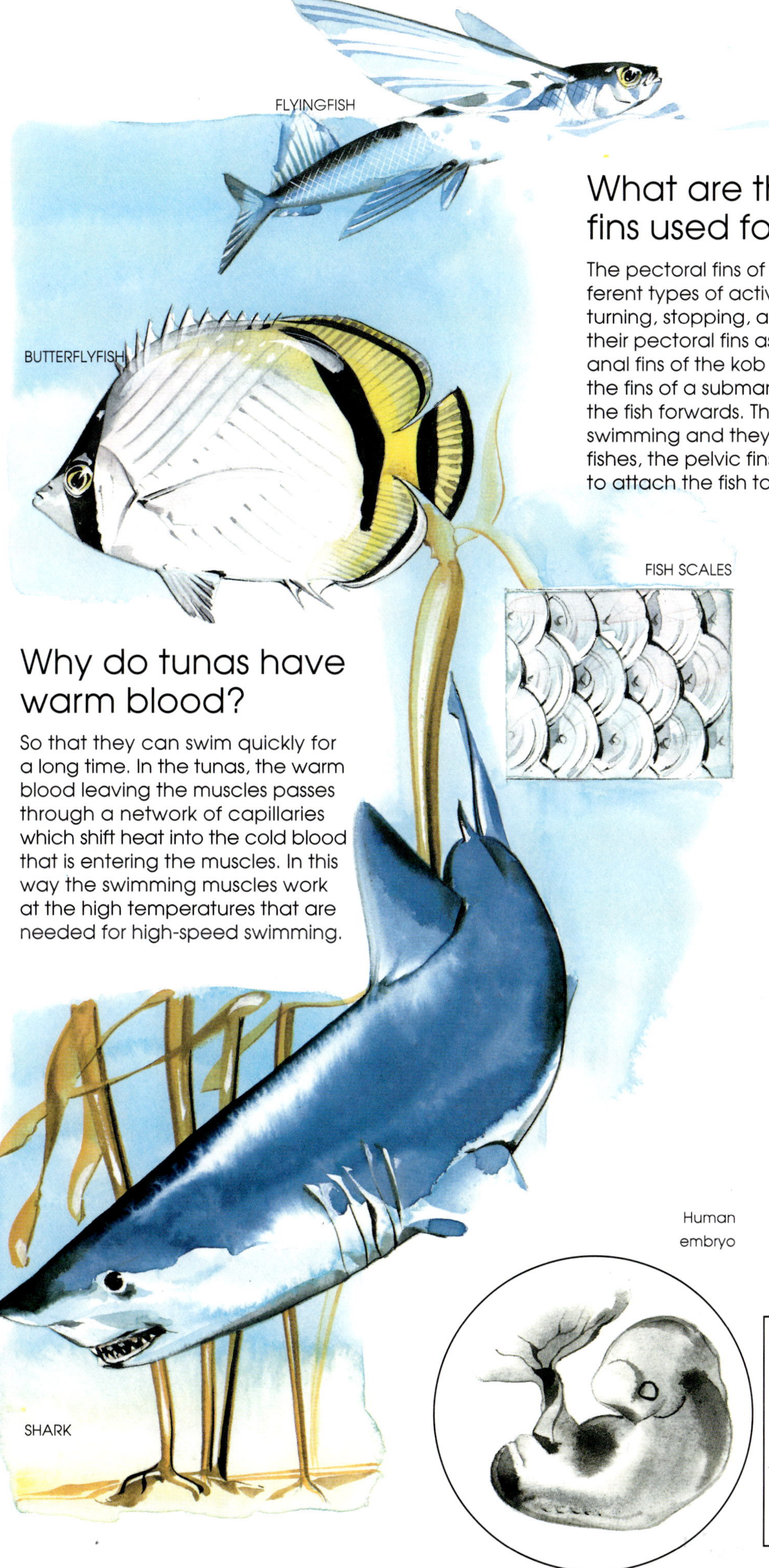

What are the different kinds of fins used for?

The pectoral fins of the butterflyfish are used for many different types of activities, such as hovering, swimming, turning, stopping, and fighting displays. Flyingfishes use their pectoral fins as 'wings' for gliding. The dorsal and anal fins of the kob keep the fish on a steady course, like the fins of a submarine, and the powerful tail fin pushes the fish forwards. The pelvic fins keep the fish level while swimming and they are also used for stopping. In clingfishes, the pelvic fins are joined to form a sucking organ to attach the fish to rocks.

Why do tunas have warm blood?

So that they can swim quickly for a long time. In the tunas, the warm blood leaving the muscles passes through a network of capillaries which shift heat into the cold blood that is entering the muscles. In this way the swimming muscles work at the high temperatures that are needed for high-speed swimming.

Why do fishes have scales?

The scales on a fish's body protect it from predators and parasites because it forms a flexible armour coating. The rows of scales bend with the swimming movements of the fish to make a smooth, streamlined body-shape over which the water flows smoothly. Some scales, which are found in a line along the middle of the body, have tiny pits that are used to measure the speed of water currents.

Are all fishes cold-blooded?

Most fishes are cold-blooded animals. This means that their body temperature is usually low and it changes with the temperature of the water. Some large, fast-swimming fishes, such as tunas, marlins, and the mako and great white sharks, keep their body temperature above that of the water temperature.

Did you know?

Unborn human babies about 28 days old look like fishes. They have simple gill openings and a tail and live in a water-filled sac inside their mother. This shows that we evolved from a fish-like animal.

FOSSIL FISH

The variety of fishes

There are many more different kinds of fishes than there are frogs, snakes and lizards, birds and mammals! Fishes first appeared in the fossil record over 100 million years before all other backboned animals, and they have always been common in seas and fresh waters. It isn't surprising that fishes are so successful as 78 per cent of the Earth's surface is covered by water. Many marine fishes live along shallow coasts but fewer species occur in deep water.

Why are there so many marine fishes?

The richness of our sea fishes is because of the incredible variety of underwater habitats which are found off the coast. These habitats range from coral reefs, rocky and sandy shores to mud flats, estuaries, lagoons, and oceans which are over 5 000 metres deep. Another reason is that South Africa is the meeting place of three great oceans – the Atlantic, Indian and Southern Oceans and has fishes from all these oceans. South Africa has more marine fish families than the Philippines or Australia, but less than Japan.

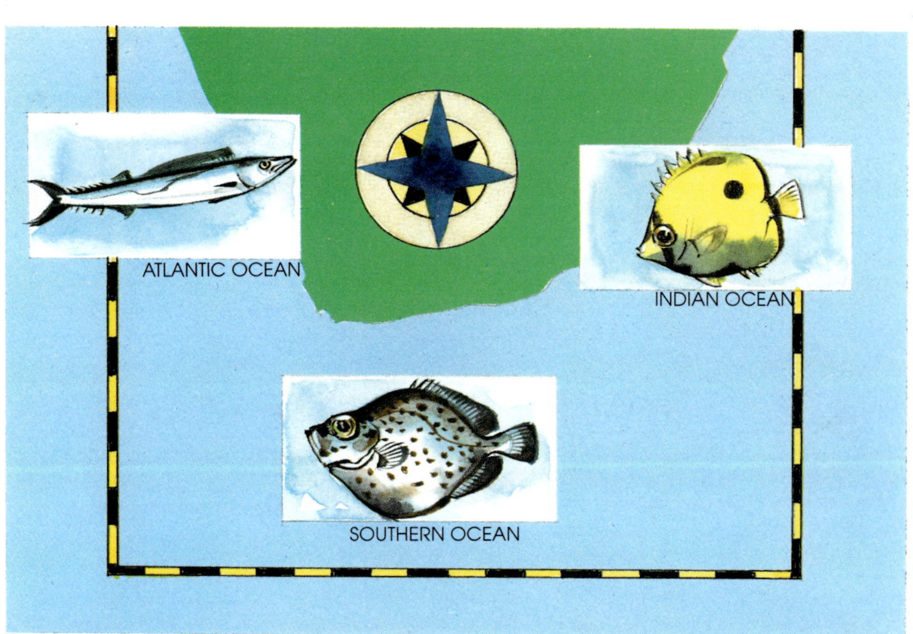

Which is the largest fish?

The plankton-eating whale shark is the largest fish. A giant, 12,65 metres long and weighing over 15 000 kilograms, was once caught off Pakistan, but they may even reach over 18 metres in length.

WHALE SHARK

How many fishes are there?

There are about 24 000 species of fishes in the world. Of these, about 15 000 live in the sea and 9 000 live in fresh waters and estuaries. Over 2 300 species of marine fishes live off the coast of southern Africa, which is about 9,6 per cent of the world's total fish fauna. About 150 species of fishes live in South African estuaries.

HUNTING FOR FISH

Are new species of fishes still being discovered?

Yes, several new species of fishes are discovered each year, some by anglers, children or holidaymakers. In 1979 Mark Pote, an18-year-old, found an interesting pufferfish in a tidal pool while on holiday in Port Alfred. He took the fish to the JLB Smith Institute of Ichthyology in Grahamstown. The scientists there found that it was a new species of fish, and so they named the fish after him.

Which is the fastest fish in southern Africa?

The sailfish, which can swim at speeds greater than 109 kilometres per hour over a short distance. This is faster than a cheetah, the fastest mammal, which can reach 96 kilometres per hour. Other fast fishes include the marlin, the wahoo, and the yellowfin tuna, as well as the swordfish and some of the larger sharks. A speeding tuna can move its tail at an amazing 10 beats per second!

SAILFISH

DWARF GOBY

Which is the smallest fish?

Gobies are the smallest fishes and the shortest backboned animals. The smallest fish in the world is a dwarf goby from Chagos archipelago which is only 8,6 millimetres long in males and 8,9 millimetres long in females. The smallest fish in southern Africa is another dwarf goby that reaches 16 millimetres in length.

Do any marine fish live only in South African waters?

Yes, at least 280 species of marine fishes in southern Africa are not found anywhere else. These indigenous fishes are mainly klipfishes, gobies, seabreams, catsharks and toadfishes. The carpenter, Fransmadam, dageraad, red stumpnose, janbruin, musselcracker and red steenbras are examples of indigenous seabreams.

RED STUMPNOSE

DAGERAAD

MUSSELCRACKER

Sharks and their cousins

Sharks, rays and chimaeras have skeletons made of cartilage. They are the lions and eagles of the sea because they feed on other sea creatures. Cartilaginous fishes can move as quickly in the water as birds do in the air, and may swim across wide stretches of ocean. They have large brains and a good sense of sight and taste. They can also detect underwater vibrations using special sense organs.

MANTA RAY

DEVILRAY

Are sharks really primitive?

No. Although the basic shapes of sharks have changed very little for millions of years, they have developed brains, skeletons, teeth and fins that are as advanced as those of the bony fishes. Among the most advanced of all fishes are the devilrays which are birdlike and have rather large brains.

How many sharks are there?

There are about 1 110 species of cartilaginous fishes in the world's oceans. Of these, about 470 species are sharks, 570 are skates and rays and 70 are chimaeras, ratfishes and elephantfishes. In southern Africa there are about 110 species of sharks, 64 skates and rays and 8 chimaeras, which is a total of 182 species of cartilaginous fishes. Sharks are even more common in Australia.

LIFE CYCLES OF SHARKS AND RAYS

GREAT WHITE SHARK

How do sharks and rays breed?

They either lay their eggs in hard cases which protect them from hungry predators or give birth to live young which can swim into hiding places. Unlike most bony fishes, sharks and rays produce only a few eggs or young – usually less than 50 each year. The young are released at birth and are not guarded by their parents. The eggs in the egg cases hatch after two to twelve months.

SHARK CAGE

Do sharks attack people?

A very small number of sharks attack people, probably because they mistake them for their natural prey. No shark will eat people as a normal part of its diet. Not many sharks found off South Africa are dangerous to humans. Of these, the three most dangerous are the great white, the Zambezi and the tiger shark. These are the same sharks that are dangerous off Australia. In KwaZulu-Natal, anti-shark nets protect swimmers from sharks.

Which is the largest shark ever?

The extinct great-tooth shark, which reached a length of 17,8 metres. This is about three times the length of a car! The largest predatory shark found in South African waters is the great white shark which reaches 7,9 metres and 3 500 kilograms. The smallest shark in South Africa is the 20-centimetre-long dwarf shark.

DWARF SHARK

Do sharks have to swim all the time to breathe?

No. Some sharks can pump water over their gills by opening and closing their mouth cavity while they are not swimming. Most of the large, fast-swimming sharks do have to keep moving so that they can take up enough oxygen from the water passing over their gills.

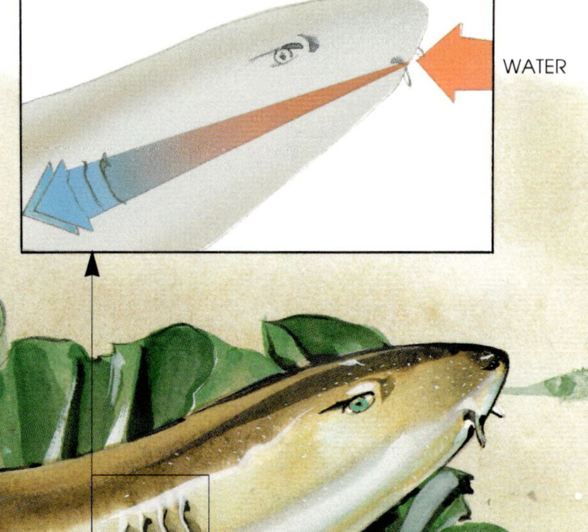

RESTING SHARK

The amazing coelacanth

DEEPSEA COELACANTHS

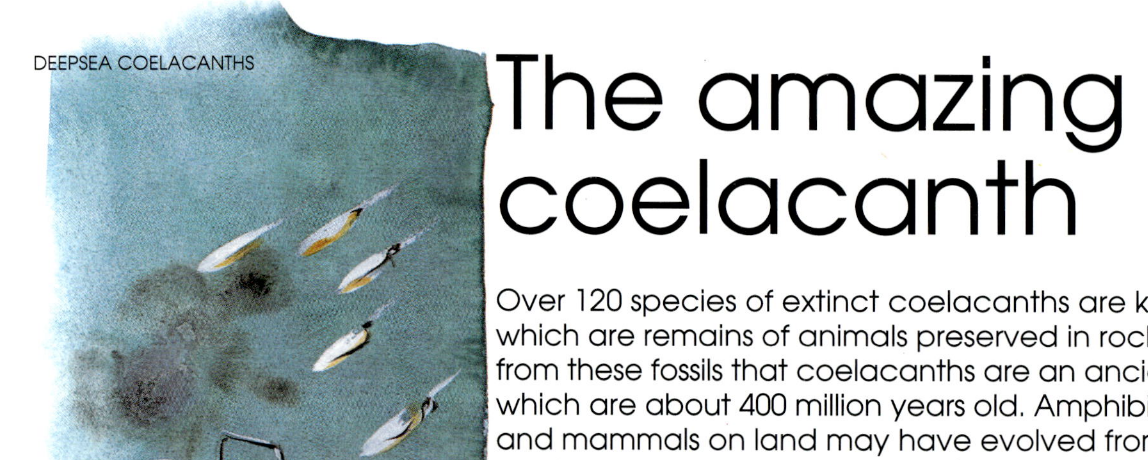

Over 120 species of extinct coelacanths are known from fossils, which are remains of animals preserved in rocks. We have learnt from these fossils that coelacanths are an ancient group of fishes which are about 400 million years old. Amphibians, reptiles, birds and mammals on land may have evolved from a relative of the coelacanth. The fossil record of this fish stopped abruptly about 65 million years ago and they were thought to have disappeared forever. It was a great surprise when a living coelacanth was caught near East London in South Africa in 1938.

How many coelacanths are there?

There may be less than 1 000 coelacanths worldwide. The German diver and scientist, Hans Fricke, counted coelacanths off the coast of Grand Comoro using a submarine designed for research and found that there are about 500 adults there. A smaller number occurs off Anjouan island. Coelacanths probably also live on the East African coast, but we are not sure how many there are.

What do coelacanths eat?

Fishes, such as reef fishes, snipe eels and small sharks, and squids. The coelacanth is a drift-hunter that glides with the current and pounces on its prey. They may find their prey by detecting the electrical signals that the prey send out. Coelacanths hunt mainly at night and shelter from their predators in caves during the day. Coelacanths are preyed on by giant sharks.

How are coelacanths caught?

All the coelacanths caught in the Comoros have been hooked on long fishing lines by local fishermen in dugout canoes or galawas who were trying to catch oilfish. Oilfish are large fish that live at the same depth as coelacanths and are valued for their flesh and oils. Coelacanths are not good to eat. Between one and 11 coelacanths are caught each year by fishermen, who go out mainly at night. The coelacanth, called 'gombessa' in the Comoros, had little value before Western scientists showed an interest in it. Conservationists are trying to lessen the fishing pressure on the coelacanth.

COELACANTH FISHERMAN

Where was the first coelacanth caught?

The first coelacanth known to scientists was caught in December 1938 in a trawl net off the Chalumna River. The second coelacanth was hooked off Anjouan island in the Comoros in 1952 and the third off Grand Comoro in 1953. Comoran fishermen have probably been catching coelacanths for centuries as over 180 of these fish have been caught off the Comoros since 1938. In August 1991 a coelacanth was caught off Mozambique near Quelimane, which tells us that coelacanths may live off the African coast.

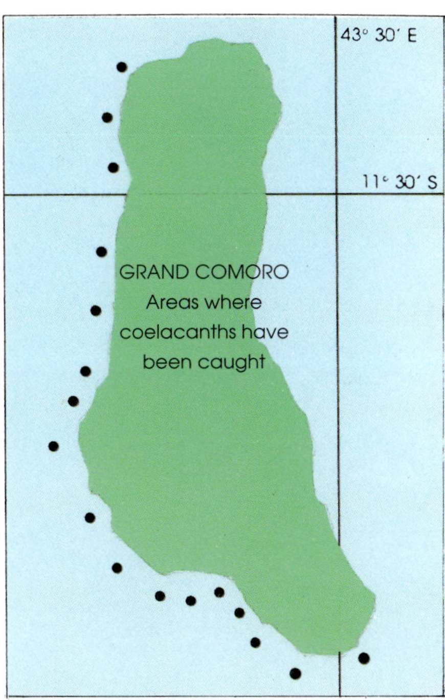

How big does a coelacanth grow?

The largest coelacanth ever recorded was about the size of a big man – 178 centimetres long and weighing 98 kilograms. This large specimen was caught off the coast of Mozambique in 1991. Another coelacanth which was caught off Grand Comoro in 1960 measured 180 centimetres and weighed 95 kilograms. Male coelacanths are smaller than the females and all the very large specimens are females. We know from the fossil record that most extinct coelacanths were small.

How do coelacanths breed?

Coelacanths do not lay eggs but give birth to live young. The developing pups absorb yolk from their large yolksacs. Oxygen and food may also pass directly from the mother to the young. The young fish are quite large at birth and as many as 26 may be born at a time!

Is the coelacanth threatened with extinction?

Yes. Their numbers are very low and they only live off a few islands in the western Indian Ocean and maybe on the African coast. If we catch too many the one remaining coelacanth species may also disappear forever. Coelacanths could also die out if we catch too many of their prey or pollute their deep water habitat. The coelacanth is one of the most beautiful and interesting fishes in the sea and it is important that we conserve it.

JUVENILE COELACANTH

THREATENED COELACANTH

Modern bony fishes

Bony fishes make up about 90 per cent of all living fishes and are the most common of all backboned animals. They typically have jaws, a bony skeleton, paired fins and two pairs of nostrils. There are three main groups of bony fishes: lungfishes, coelacanths and rayfinned fishes. The bony fishes first evolved about 500 million years ago and have diversified into a bewildering array of forms. Many fishes that are familiar to us, such as sardines, trouts, eels, kobs, marlins, gobies and most tropical reef fishes, are bony fishes.

Which is the deadliest fish?

Probably the stonefish, which is well camouflaged and has several dorsal spines with sacs of neurotoxic venom at their bases. An unwary wader or swimmer who stands on the spines may be injected with poison, which is very painful and often fatal. The stonefish is found in the Red Sea and in tropical parts of the Pacific and Indian Oceans as far south as Durban. The lionfish and eel-catfish are less dangerous fishes but we still have to be careful when we handle them as they have poison in their fin spines.

What is countershading?

Fishes living in the well-lit open waters of the sea, such as kingfishes and needlefishes, are countershaded to disguise their shape and to blend in with the featureless background light of the sea. When they are looked at from above, their dark backs match the colour of the deep ocean. Seen from below, they look like silvery streaks against a mirror.

What is a rocksucker?

The rocksucker is a kind of giant clingfish that lives close to the shore and can sometimes be found attached to rocks in crevices above water at low tide. Their pelvic fins are formed into a large sucking disc which they use to attach themselves to rocks so that they are not washed away. They have two prominent teeth which are used to lever sea urchins and limpets off the rocks. Their dried-up carcasses are sometimes found on the beach.

How do fishes produce their silvery colour?

The silvery, shiny colours of fishes, such as sardines, are produced in special cells in the skin. These cells, called iridocytes, contain crystals of guanin arranged in layers which reflect the different colours of light. Guanin taken from fishes is used to make silver paint.

How do fishes change colour?

The non-shiny colours of fishes are produced in pigment cells called chromatophores. Each cell contains a different colour pigment (yellow, red, orange, black, etc). The pigment granules can be moved around in the cell. When the pigment is spread throughout the cell the colour is brighter, but when the granules are concentrated the brightness is lessened. The contraction and expansion of the pigments brings about the changes in colour pattern, for example, when a Cape stumpnose changes from a silvery colour to silver with dark crossbars at night.

Why do fishes change colour?

To match different backgrounds and to send messages to other fishes. A galjoen, for example, is dark when it swims among rocks but changes to a paler colour when it swims over sand. Soles and flounders have an amazing ability to change colour so that they are camouflaged against different colour backgrounds. When fishes are breeding or fighting they may have brighter colours. Fishes often have different colour patterns during the day and at night, and may show the night pattern if they are frightened during the day. Young fishes, such as the African coris, have completely different colours from the adults.

Fish shapes and structures

We usually think of fishes as silver, slippery, streamlined animals but most are quite different from this description. Many fishes have long bodies whereas others are short and deep. Some are round whereas others are flattened. The fins may form complicated shapes or may not even be present at all. Fishes have probably adopted a greater variety of shapes and sizes than any other group of backboned animals.

MUDHOPPERS

Can fishes breathe air?

Most fishes remove oxygen from the water using their gills, but some are able to breathe air. The ability to breathe air is highly developed in some freshwater fishes. The lungfishes, for example, have both gills and lungs. Some marine fishes are also able to breathe air. The mudhopper, which waddles around on mudflats in mangrove swamps, breathes through its skin. Mullet that are trapped in warm, stagnant water often jump out of the water to take in air which is then kept in bubbles in a chamber above the gills.

Why do fish have swimbladders?

Swimbladders help fishes to float in midwater. Gas is pumped in or out to change the buoyancy. If a fish is pulled too quickly to the surface, the gas in the bladder cannot adjust quickly enough to the decreasing pressure. The bladder then either bursts or pushes the internal organs out through the mouth. Some fishes have lost their swimbladders or they have become filled with fat. The bladders of coelacanths are filled with lipids or low density oils.

SWIMBLADDER FORCED THROUGH MOUTH

What is the lateral line?

The lateral line is a sense organ that runs along the head and body of a fish and is used to pick up low frequency sound or other vibrations in the water. The kob has a lateral line that is easy to see. The small sensory organs or hair cells in the lateral line are sensitive to the vibrations that are caused by fishes swimming nearby. By listening to one another using their lateral line organs, shoaling fishes such as anchovies are able to swim in tight formation and avoid bumping into each other in a school.

How do fishes produce sounds?

The swimbladder is used by some fishes to make or amplify sounds. Muscles which are attached to the gas-filled swimbladder are contracted to produce sound waves that are heard as growls, yelps, whistles, grunts, hoots and drumming noises. These noises are either used to chase away predators or to attract mates. Grunters and kobs are well known fishes that produce sounds. Male rat-tails use special muscles to make a drumming sound on their swimbladder to attract the female. Once you have learned how to listen underwater, you will find that the sea is not a silent world at all!

BULL SHARK

SAWFISH

Can marine fishes live in fresh water?

Some sea fishes, such as bull sharks, sawfishes, glassies, silversides, sleepers, gobies, moonies, mullets and kobs are able to survive in estuaries and rivers. This is because these fishes can tolerate wide changes in salt concentrations, or salinity, from 35 parts per thousand (sea water) to 0 parts per thousand (fresh water). The Mozambique tilapia, which is normally a freshwater fish, is so tolerant of sea water that it has even been found breeding in the sea. Zambezi sharks and sawfishes have been caught in rivers hundreds of kilometres upstream of the estuary.

Why doesn't the blood of Antarctic fishes freeze?

Some, like the bullhead notothen, have 'anti-freeze' chemicals in their blood which stop them from freezing in the -1 degree to -2 degrees Celsius water temperatures in which they live. The freezing point of fish blood is -1,2 degrees Celsius but the anti-freezes lower the freezing point to -2,2 degrees Celsius. Anti-freezes are found in about 15 species of notothens in the Southern Ocean.

Did you know?

Scientists have found that the slightly rough skin of a shark allows water to flow over it more smoothly than over a completely smooth skin. Modern aircraft wings and bodies have now been designed with the same slightly rough surface so that they can fly more smoothly through the air.

BULLHEAD NOTOTHEN

Senses of fishes

The sense organs of fishes pick up physical or chemical signals in the water. Changes in water temperature or touch are felt through skin receptors. Light signals are received through the eyes, and sounds or vibrations are picked up through the inner ear or lateral line. Chemical stimuli are picked up by the smell or taste organs.

HOOKED ROMAN

Do fishes feel pain?

When a Roman is caught on a hook and line, it can definitely feel through its nervous system that it has been hooked, and will try to escape. Unlike humans, most fishes have no frontal lobe in their primitive brains and so they are not likely to be distressed by any pain that they feel. It is nevertheless cruel to cut open or otherwise damage a fish that is still alive.

Can fishes smell?

Yes, a goatfish can smell even the smallest traces of chemicals in the water or in the sand using its sense cells. The sense of smell is used to trace prey, to find mates, to avoid danger and to find familiar places. Sharks and rays have a very good sense of smell. Some fishes, such as sea catfish, rely more on smell than sight to find their prey. Mullet use their sense of smell to find their way from the sea to estuaries.

GOATFISH

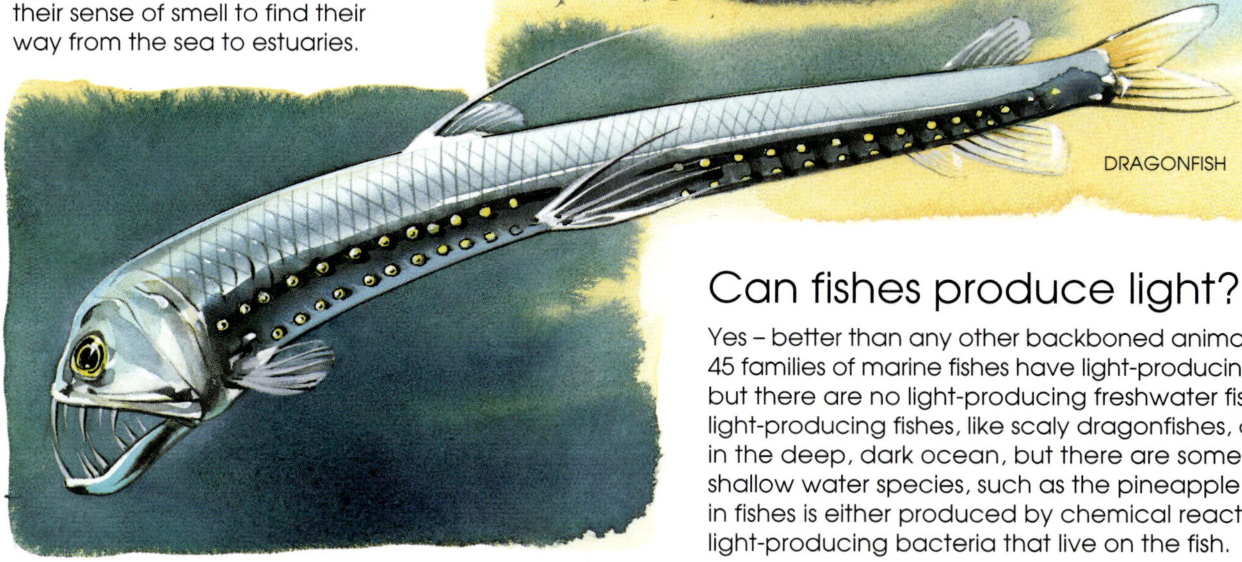

DRAGONFISH

Can fishes produce light?

Yes – better than any other backboned animals! At least 45 families of marine fishes have light-producing species, but there are no light-producing freshwater fishes. Most light-producing fishes, like scaly dragonfishes, are found in the deep, dark ocean, but there are some luminous shallow water species, such as the pineapple fish. Light in fishes is either produced by chemical reactions or by light-producing bacteria that live on the fish.

Why do fishes produce light?

Deepsea anglerfish have light organs suspended on long tendrils which they dangle in the water to attract unsuspecting prey. The scaleless dragonfishes, for example, find their prey using headlights that produce a red light which their prey cannot see. The viperfish has lights inside its mouth to attract prey. Dim lights on the body of a fish camouflage it as they break up its outline. Many fishes have patterns of lights on their bodies that are different from those of other fishes so that their mates can recognise them.

Which fish uses a flashlight?

The flashlight fish has a large light-producing organ under the eye where there is a colony of millions of bacteria. The light organ is switched off by turning it downwards into a black pocket under the eye. The lights are used to confuse predators. When it sees an attacker the flashlight fish swims in a straight line then suddenly closes off its light, changes direction and rushes away.

FLASHLIGHT FISH

Can fish see colour?

Yes, many species of shallow water fishes, such as parrotfishes, wrasses, angelfishes and butterflyfishes, can see different colours. Fishes that live in well-lit, shallow waters, like the longnose butterflyfish, have mainly cone cells in the retina of their eyes so that they can clearly see colours. Deepsea fishes, like eelpouts, have mainly rod cells in their retinas so that they can see at low light levels. Many deepsea fishes are colour blind. In the deepest parts of the oceans fishes have tiny eyes or are completely blind.

EEL-CATFISH

Do fishes really detect electrical signals?

Sharks, rays and many bony fishes, such as the eel-catfish, have electrical sense organs that can detect the electrical fields of other animals. Sharks and rays living on the sea bottom have many electrical sense organs in their heads and find prey buried in the sand or at night using these electroreceptors. Some fishes may even use their electric organs to navigate during long journeys through the ocean by following the magnetic field of the Earth.

Can fishes stun their prey?

The marbled electric ray uses strong electrical discharges made in special kidney-shaped organs on each side of the body to stun its prey. Anglers, divers and swimmers receive a nasty shock if they stand on these fishes! Torpedo rays can give off a 220-volt shock and electric catfishes in fresh water can give off an even more deadly 300-volt shock.

Where fishes live

Water is everything to fishes. It is their freeway, nursery, school, playground, house, toilet and grave. Fishes live in the deepest parts of the oceans and in cold lakes on top of mountains. Fishes can also be found in freshwater lakes and in lagoons where the salt content is three times higher than sea water. From this we can see that fishes thrive in the cold Arctic and Antarctic as well as in hot tropical lakes and rivers. They also live in underground waters and cave lakes.

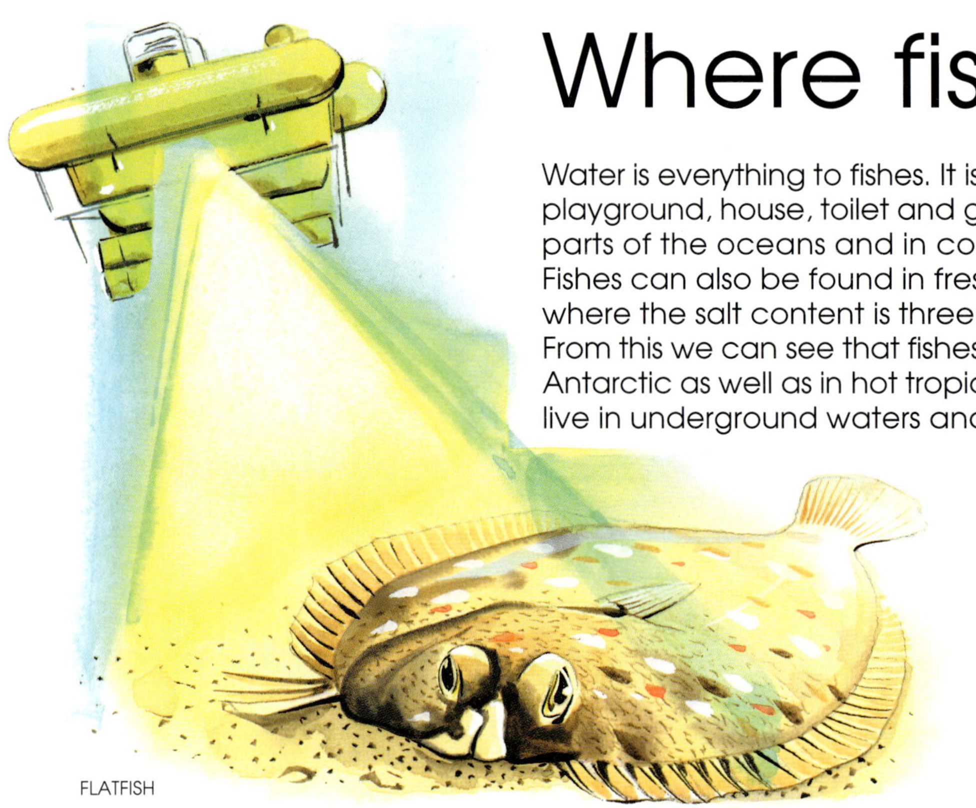
FLATFISH

How deep do fishes live?

Fishes have been seen from research submarines in the deepest parts of the oceans. A flatfish was found at a depth of 10 911 metres near the bottom of the Mariana Trench in the Pacific Ocean. The average depth of the oceans is over 1 500 metres and most fish like to live in the shallower half where there is more food.

Why is the pearlfish not a welcome guest?

They live inside a sea cucumber! The sea cucumber tries to stop the pearlfish from entering its body, but when it opens its breathing hole, the pearlfish slips in tail first and rests with its head poking out. The pearlfish sometimes eats parts of the internal organs of the sea cucumber, so it is not very welcome.

PEARLFISH IN A SEA CUCUMBER

Are sharks really the monsters of the deep?

No, not all are. In fact, most sharks, such as dogfishes and rays, live in shallow water around the edge of the ocean but some live in the surf zone, or in water deeper than 3 000 metres. Sharks can be found in the tropics and, less commonly, in cool and cold oceans. Some sharks are active by day, and others by night. Some live by themselves whereas others live in groups.

DOGFISH

RAY

Are there any sessile fishes?

Yes, garden eels are sessile fishes because they stay in one place throughout their adult lives. They live tail-down in a hole in the sand in colonies or groups. Garden eels sway gently to and fro in the current while they wait for small prey to drift past them. When they are frightened, they slip backwards into their burrows.

Can fishes live in hot springs?

Yes. Some freshwater fishes that live in hot springs feel comfortable in temperatures which reach higher than 40 degrees Celsius! This is even hotter than a hot bath! Fishes in the Antarctic and Arctic live at near freezing temperatures, but most fishes live in water that is warmer than10 degrees and cooler than 30 degrees Celsius.

Why do some fishes live with shrimps?

The pinkbar goby, like many other gobies, lives in a burrow with a shrimp so that it can share housekeeping duties. The goby digs the burrow and catches prey. The shrimp eats the scraps of left-over food and cleans out the burrow. Both the shrimp and the goby keep a lookout for predators.

Did you know?

African mudhoppers are fishes that spend most of their lives out of water! They live in muddy mangrove swamps and waddle around on the mud looking for small crabs and worms to eat. Mudhoppers are able to stay out of water for long periods as they can breathe air through their skin and modified gills. They can also take up oxygen through their tails and you will notice, if you observe them carefully, that they sometimes let their tails dangle in a pool of water so that they can breathe through them!

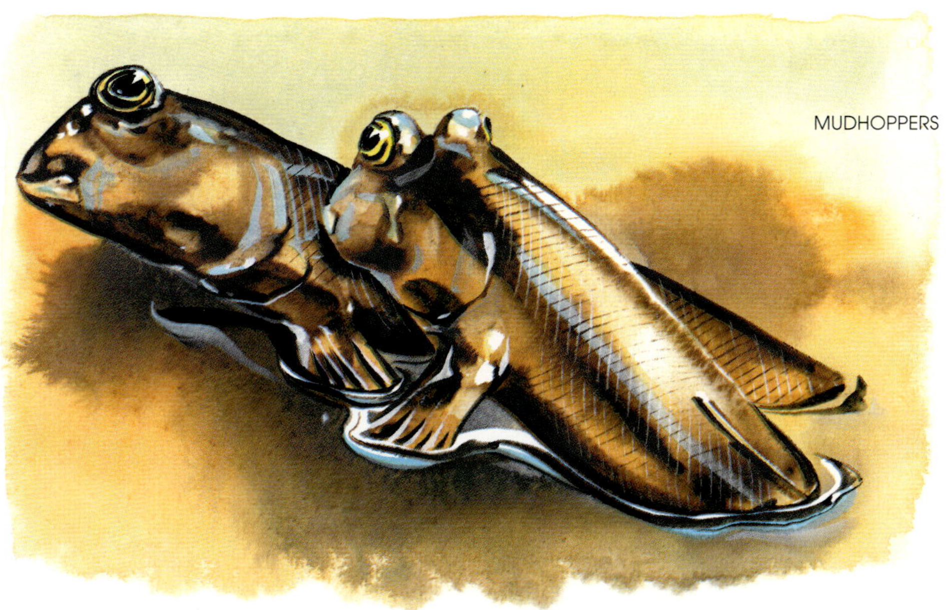

Raising a family

Most fishes hatch from small eggs. These eggs are scattered in open water and are not protected by the parents. Some fishes lay eggs in nests or crevices where they are guarded by their parents. A smaller group of advanced fishes are bearers. This means that their eggs hatch inside the mother's body. When the small juvenile fishes are born, they look like the adults. Fishes which do not guard their young usually lay large numbers of small eggs but guarders and bearers lay fewer, larger eggs and give birth to large young.

OCEAN SUNFISH

Which fish produces millions of eggs?

The ocean sunfish lays over 30 million small eggs each time it breeds! The reason why this fish can lay so many eggs is because of its huge size. It is over three metres long and weighs about 2 800 kilograms. They swim in the open ocean, often near the surface, and feed on jellyfish and large zooplankton. Baby sunfishes look very different from the adults and were once thought to be a different species.

Which fish lays the least eggs?

The fewest eggs are produced by a mouthbrooding fish from Lake Tanganyika which lays seven or less eggs each time it breeds. A pregnant coelacanth caught in the Comoros in 1962 contained only five developing young but other coelacanths have had as many as 26 fertilised eggs. The egg of the coelacanth is about the size of an orange and is the largest egg of any fish.

Where do freshwater eels breed?

In the open sea. When the large eels that live in our rivers are ready to breed, they swim down to the sea and then carry out a remarkable journey all the way to the western Indian Ocean where they breed. The larval eels, called leptocephali, drift southwards with the currents and change into tiny, transparent glass eels which enter our rivers during summer. Once in the river, the glass eel becomes coloured and, as an elver, swims to the top of the river, where it lives for 10 to 15 years.

FRESHWATER EELS

Do manta rays give birth by jumping out of the water?

Probably. It is known that manta rays give birth to live young. At least two people, one in South Africa and one in California, have seen giant manta rays jump out of the water and fling their newly-born young into the air. Their normal method of giving birth is probably in the water. If you see a manta ray jump out of the water, keep a careful watch for any young that might be born!

Why do some fishes change sex?

A sex change helps a fish produce more young. If it is one sex (for example, a female) when it is small and changes into the other sex (male) when it is large, then it can mate with the other females and have more young. Many species of marine fishes change sex during their life cycles. About 20 of the 40 species of seabreams in southern Africa change sex, either from males to females or from females to males. The Roman, a common angling species, changes from a female that lives in groups to a male that lives by itself during its life cycle.

Do male seahorses give birth?

No, but it does seem as if he does because the female places her eggs in a pouch on the male's body. It is then the male seahorse's job to protect the developing eggs and juveniles in the pouch until they are large enough to fend for themselves. There are six species of seahorses in southern Africa. The Knysna seahorse, which lives in lagoons and estuaries along the southern Cape coast, may die out if we do not take better care of its environment.

MALE SEAHORSE

How do sea catfish care for their young?

The males care for the eggs and young in their mouths. The eggs are the size of small marbles and hatch in the mouth. The young fishes swim out of their father's mouth to feed but scurry back when danger threatens. Cardinal fishes also care for their eggs and young in their mouths.

Feeding and growing

Fishes, like all animals, need food in order to survive and grow. Some fishes feed entirely on plants and others feed only on animals, including other fishes. Some fishes feed on both plants and animals. Many fishes filter out plankton, the microscopic plants and animals that float in the sea, and others feed on micro-organisms in the bottom mud. Worms, coral polyps, snails, crabs and shrimps are important food items for fishes.

HATCHETFISH

DRAGONFISH

GULPER EEL

LANTERNFISH

What do deepsea fishes eat?

Some deepsea fishes, such as the eelpouts, feed on snails, crabs and bristleworms which themselves feed in the bottom mud on the remains of plants and animals that drift down into the depths from the well-lit surface layers. Other deepsea fishes are ambush predators which creep up on other fishes in the dark and attack. As the deep ocean is permanently dark, many deepsea fishes are blind.

EELPOUT

How does the gulper eel feed?

Because food is hard to find in the dark depths, each meal has to last a long time. Gulper eels have enormous mouths for swallowing fishes as large as themselves. They swim slowly with their jaws stretched wide open in order to catch prey. There is a light on the tip of the tail which attracts the prey closer.

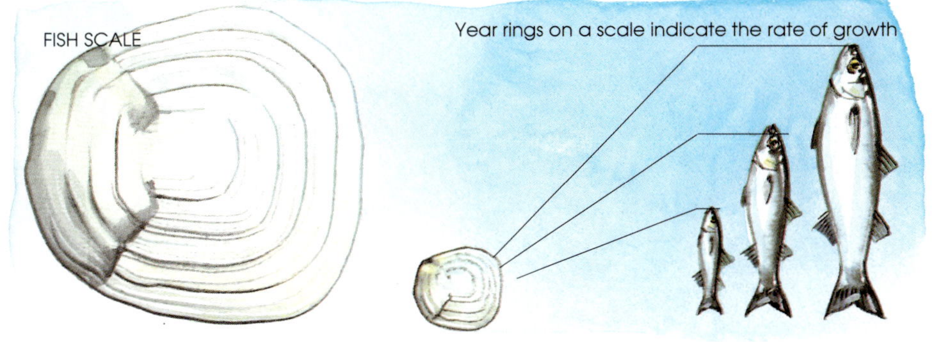

How do you tell the age of a fish?

By counting the rings on its scales, otoliths (ear bones) or fin spines. Many fishes lay down one ring each year but some lay down more than one ring each year, so working out the age is not always easy! In some fishes daily growth rings are laid down on the ear bones. Once we know the age of a fish we are also able to say how quickly it grows and how old it gets.

How long do fishes live?

Larger fishes usually live longer than smaller ones. Very small gobies may only live for one or two years. Most marine fishes live for three to eight years but large sharks, groupers and rockcods can live longer than 25 years! Tunas and billfishes grow very quickly and probably do not live longer than 15 years. The coelacanth grows slowly and can probably live as long as 60 years.

AGES OF FISHES

Do fishes grow all the time?

Yes, fishes grow all their lives but they grow slower as they become older. The kob grows at a rate of 15 to 20 centimetres each year while it is young and reaches a length of 75 centimetres after four years. Later in life they grow at less than 10 centimetres a year. When they are 16 years old they are about 150 centimetres long.

The arms race

One of the laws of the sea is eat or be eaten! Predators are constantly chasing prey and prey are always on the lookout for the predator. Predators make use of speed and stealth, camouflage and pack hunting as well as large teeth and a wide gape as a way of catching a meal! Prey find ways of protecting themselves and so make it harder to be caught. They rely on speed and camouflage, as well as hiding and shoaling behaviour to stay alive. Prey may also be protected by bizarre spines, armour plating and poisons in the never-ending battle with their enemies.

HUMPBACK WHALE

Which marine animal catches fishes with a bubble net?

The humpback whale. The whale swims in a circle underneath a shoal of fishes, letting out a stream of bubbles from its blowhole. The fishes are surrounded by a 'net' of glistening bubbles and, although they could swim through it, they become confused and remain inside the 'net' where they are caught by the whale.

Can fish change colour?

Yes. Many fishes are masters of camouflage and can change their colour, like a chameleon, so that they match their background. At night, the fusilier fish sleeps near the sea bed and is darkly coloured to match its background. During the day it swims up into the bright surface waters to feed and changes to a pale, translucent colour.

FUSILIER FISH

Why does the porcupinefish blow itself up?

When a porcupinefish is surprised by a predator it swallows water and blows itself up to the size of a small football. The spines on the body stick out and most attackers are either scared off or are unable to swallow their prey. Dried, blown-up porcupinefishes are used as lampshades and ornaments.

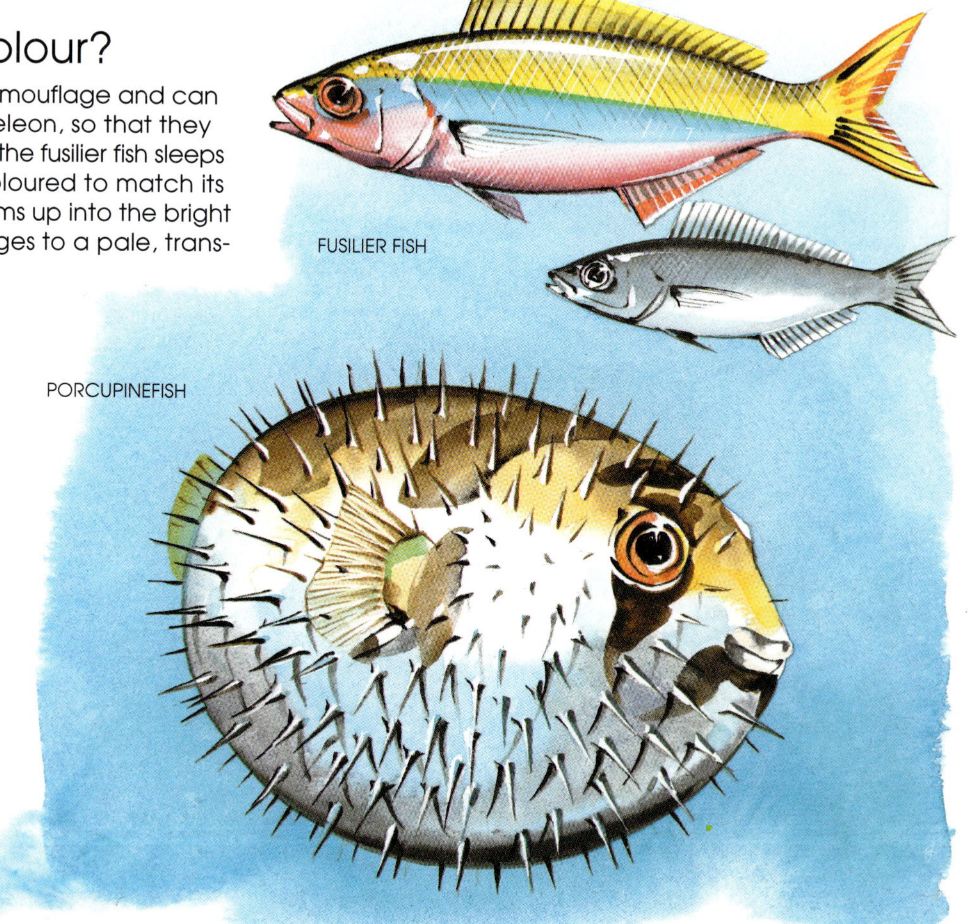

PORCUPINEFISH

Are any fishes poisonous?

Yes, there are several poisonous fishes. The liver, reproductive organs, muscles and intestine of puffers are very poisonous and other fish will not eat them. In Japan, people eat the puffer, which is regarded as a delicacy, but an expert chef must first remove the poisonous organs and make the flesh safe. Still, the puffer or fugu continues to kill people every year in Japan. The liver of the red steenbras, and probably of tunas and some sharks, shouldn't be eaten because, like the livers of the seal and the polar bear, they have a very high vitamin A content. Eating their livers may result in nausea and stomach cramps.

Why are some fish brightly coloured?

Puffer fishes are brightly coloured to warn predators that they are poisonous or not very tasty. Butterflyfishes use their bright colours to attract mates. In some fishes, bright colours are used to show aggression or submission or to frighten off rivals for mates or territories. Many fishes have five or more colour patterns to suit their different moods.

Can fishes really fly?

Flyingfishes swim near the water surface. When a predator attacks they project themselves out of the water at speed and spread their broad fins out to glide rather than fly. They take off at about 64 kilometres per hour and can glide for over 1 000 metres. They confuse most of their predators by gliding through the air but dolphinfish are able to follow their flight paths and catch the flyingfish as they flop back into the water.

Did you know?

There are several kinds of fishes in South Africa with poisonous spines, including stingrays, catfishes, rabbitfishes, scorpionfishes, stonefishes, turkeyfishes and firefishes. Turkeyfishes, though small and slow-moving, can be quite aggressive and have been known to attack a swimmer. They occur along the east and south coast – admire them but beware!

LANTERNFISHES

Peculiar behaviour

People have been interested in how fishes behave ever since they started to catch them for food. Feeding and breeding are the most important behaviour of fishes. Feeding is essential for the survival of individual fishes and breeding enables the fish to have offspring, making sure that the species survives. Other behaviour, such as avoiding predators, help the fish to remain healthy and safe when it is not feeding and breeding.

Why do fishes migrate?

Migrations are regular mass movements of fishes from one place to another, usually to feed or breed. These migrations take place along the coast or from deep to shallow water. The elf migrates from KwaZulu-Natal to the southern Cape coast in late summer and returns to KwaZulu-Natal in spring. Lanternfishes migrate several hundred metres upwards into shallow water each evening to feed on the plankton.

What is the sardine run?

Sardines or pilchards are cool water fishes that normally live off the southern and western Cape. During winter, a band of cool water forms along the coasts of the eastern Cape and KwaZulu-Natal and the sardines, together with anchovies and round herrings, migrate northwards, perhaps to find new feeding grounds. They are sometimes washed onto the beaches in large numbers and are caught by local people.

Shark

REMORA

Do fishes hitchhike?

Yes. The remora is a hitchhiking scavenger that attaches itself by a sucker to large fish, such as sharks or manta rays, as well as to dolphins, turtles and even ships! When its host finds food, the remora lets go and feeds on the scraps. The remora attaches itself using a vacuum sucker which has ridges on it to stop it from being detached from its host unless it swims forward. Another hitchhiker is the male anglerfish, which is far smaller than the female and attaches itself to her for life. When she lays her eggs the male is nearby to fertilise them.

What do cleaner fish eat?

They remove parasites and dead skin from large fishes. The cleaners work inside the mouths and gills as well as over the bodies of their 'patients'. Both fishes benefit as the cleaner obtains a free meal and the large fish gets rid of its parasites. The cleaner fish perform peculiar dances that enable the large fish to identify them. Several wrasses are cleaners when they are young but feed on coral polyps as adults. Coral shrimps also act as cleaners, especially for moray eels.

What does a mimic do?

A mimic imitates another fish and is either protected or obtains food through mimicry. The sabre-toothed blenny closely resembles a cleaner wrasse and swims in a similar way. Large fish are fooled by the mimic and allow it to come close. The blenny then takes a small bite of flesh from the unsuspecting fish. Some wrasses are fish-eating predators that change colour and mimic harmless plant-eating fishes. They approach prey by swimming in a shoal of harmless fishes until they are close enough to dart out and catch their prey.

Why is the clownfish safe from the tentacles of an anemone?

A special secretion protects the clownfish from the stings of the sea anemone. The clownfish lives among the anemone's tentacles, where it is safe from predators. In return, the clownfish attracts other fish which dart into the tentacles where they are caught by the anemone. This is a good example of symbiosis, which means living together so that both partners benefit.

Do fishes sleep?

Yes, they do but without closing their eyes! Many fishes rest on the bottom or in caves and crevices at night, depending on whether they have fed during the day. Others sleep during the day but hunt at night. The parrotfish forms an amazing mucous envelope around it when it sleeps. Many wrasses bury themselves in the sand at night to sleep.

PARROTFISH

KNYSNA SEAHORSE

Conservation of fishes

Large numbers of plants and animals live along the shallow edge of the sea. The open ocean, in contrast, doesn't have much life, so it is rather like a semi-desert and the deep ocean is like a desert. Fishes were once thought to exist in huge numbers but we know now that they can easily be overfished by Man. Because we live on land we have been less concerned about conservation in the water. It is also difficult to study life under water and we are not sure how many fishes are threatened or endangered by our activities.

Are there any threatened marine fishes in South Africa?

Yes! There are at least nine marine and estuarine fishes which live in South African waters that are endangered, vulnerable or rare throughout their world range. The coelacanth, great white shark, Knysna seahorse, and bearded eelgoby may become extinct if we do not look after them more carefully. The freshwater mullet, golden sleeper, checked goby, barebreast goby and burrowing goby are very rare and also need protection. Sadly, the river pipefish has recently become extinct in South Africa.

What threatens our fish populations?

Overfishing, pollution, interference with ecological processes and changes to their habitat are the main reasons why fishes have become scarcer. Many people don't seem to care. Anglers, aquarists, commercial fishermen, divers and holidaymakers all need to work together to conserve fishes. You can help too! Learn as much as you can about fishes from books and field observations, then share your knowledge and fascination with others. Also learn about the rules of angling, bait collection and using a beach, and stay within the law. Visit oceanaria and museums to learn about fishes. Support conservation groups that campaign against pollution, environmental disturbance and overfishing.

DIVER WITH FISH

FISH BEING RELEASED

How can anglers conserve fish?

Many anglers are strong supporters of conservation. They catch only as many fish as they need, and tag and release some of their catch. They co-operate in the fish research programmes of local museums, research institutes and universities. They are aware that lead sinkers, which are often lost while fishing, may pollute the water. They use a new biodegradable sinker that decomposes into fish food after five months underwater. Other anglers use small bags of sand as sinkers. Many anglers avoid using stainless steel hooks as they do not rust quickly underwater like ordinary hooks. Hooks that do not rust are a constant threat to underwater life. Anglers who care about the environment do not throw plastic or oil into the water.

What is an alien fish?

A fish that has been introduced by Man into areas beyond its natural range. Alien fishes may damage natural communities by feeding on local fishes, introducing parasites and diseases, breeding with local fishes, disturbing the habitat and interfering with the territories of local fishes. As far as possible, communities of fishes and other animals that evolved together should not be disrupted by the introduction of alien species. Don't release your aquarium fish into the wild – it is illegal!

ALIEN CRAB

Did you know?

The Tsitsikamma National Park on the southern Cape coast is the oldest marine reserve in Africa. The Park was established in 1964 and stretches for 72 kilometres along the coast and for five kilometres out to sea. Many important angling fishes and shellfishes feed and breed in the Park. Some of these fishes then swim into overfished areas on either side of the Park and so restock these waters.

Are there any alien marine fishes in southern Africa?

Not yet, as far as we know, but they are likely to be introduced if we are not careful. There are alien fishes on the east and west coasts of North America as well as in Europe and Japan. Many of these fishes were introduced in the water that ships carry to weigh them down when they have no cargo (ballast water). Alien crabs, mussels and snails have been introduced into South Africa and have caused considerable disruptions to natural marine communities.

Could I find a new species of fish?

Yes. Many new species of fishes have been found by children, holidaymakers or anglers who knew enough about fishes to recognise that their specimen was different, and took it to a local scientist to be identified. If you find a new species of fish it may even be named after you! Whenever you are at the beach you have a chance of discovering something new.

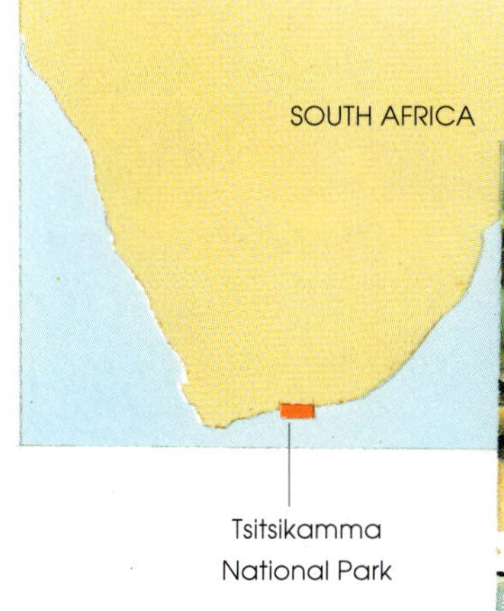

Seabirds

Although seabirds all breed on land, they depend on the sea for their food and so are very important in the marine food chain. They have many different ways of catching their prey. They may dive or swim after fish, or even pick shellfish or other small animals off the rocks. All seabirds are adapted in unique ways for their particular lifestyle.

FLAMINGOS

Which bird walks in circles for its food?

The flamingo. It feeds in shallow lakes and estuaries by shuffling its feet around in a circle to stir up the mud. As the small organisms living in the mud swarm to the surface, the flamingo holds its bill upside down in the water and moves its thick tongue to and fro. This action sucks water through the bill, which is lined with a fringe of hairs. The organisms are trapped against this fringe, from where they are licked off and swallowed.

Are kelp gulls really thieves?

Yes. They steal each other's food because it is easier than searching for their own. They often run after each other on the ground, trying to tear food from each other's beaks. Some are even more sneaky. Kelp gulls feed on mussels, which they crack open by dropping them from the air onto the rocks below. Often another gull will swoop down and steal the mussel before its owner can land.

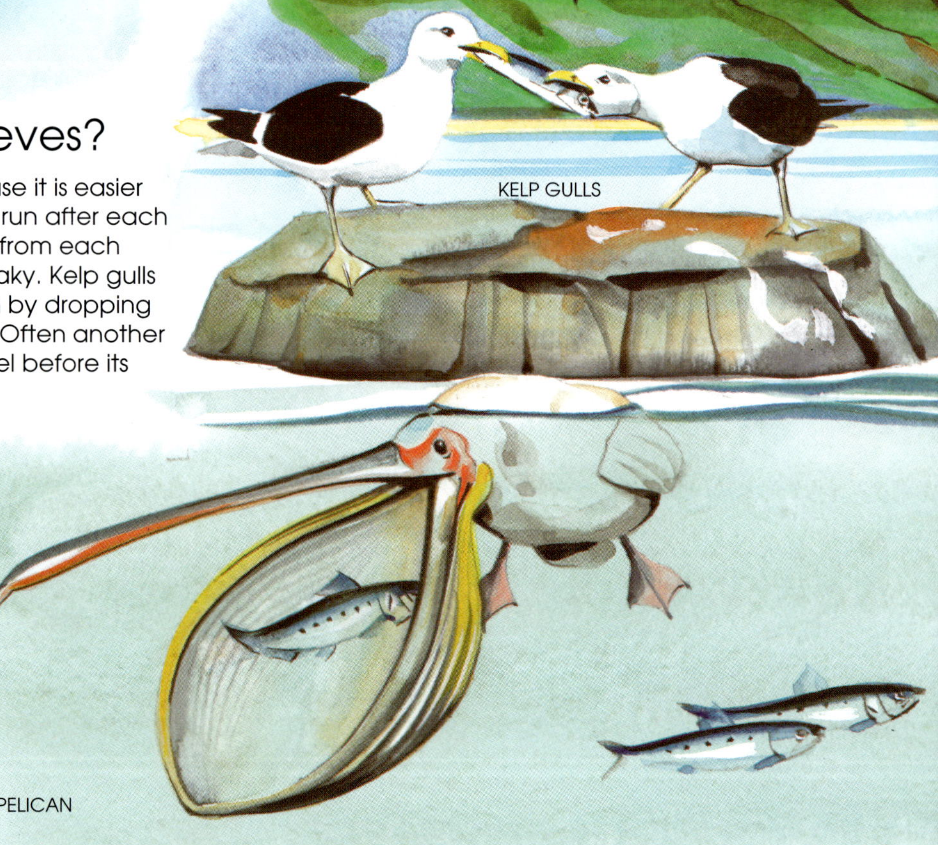

KELP GULLS

PELICAN

Why does the pelican have a throat pouch?

To scoop up fish. When the pelican chases a fish it opens its beak underwater and the pouch balloons out to surround the prey. The pelican lifts its head out of the water and tilts its beak down to drain out all the water, before throwing back its head and swallowing the fish.

Which bird dive-bombs fish?

The gannet. It dives for fish from as high as 30 metres in the air, and hits the sea with great force. The gannet has a number of adaptations for this diving habit. The bones in the skull are strengthened to absorb some of the impact when the bird hits the water, and the neck and throat area are cushioned by air sacs below the skin which are filled with air before the dive. The horny coverings over the nasal openings prevent water from being forced into them, while the eyes are protected by membranes which flick over them as soon as the bird hits the water.

Do oystercatchers only eat oysters?

No. In fact their favourite foods are mussels and limpets. By jabbing between the two halves of a mussel shell with their sharp beak, the oystercatchers can cut through the muscle which holds the two halves together. They then use their beaks like scissors to open the mussels so that they can eat the flesh inside. Oystercatchers prise limpets off the rocks by using the beak as a lever, but if the limpet won't budge they hit the edge of the shell with their closed beak to dislodge the limpet.

Do cormorants drip-dry?

Yes. The feathers of cormorants are less waterproof than those of other seabirds. This means that cormorants cannot stay in the water for very long, as their feathers become waterlogged, allowing the bird to get cold. After swimming and diving after prey, such as crabs and fish, they dry themselves off by standing on the rocks with their wings stretched out.

Do penguins fly underwater?

Yes. Although their wings are too short for flying through the air, penguins chase fish underwater by flapping their wings to propel themselves rapidly forward. Their bodies are streamlined, which helps to make them fast swimmers, and they have webbed feet which are used for steering.

Index

Struik Publishers (Pty) Ltd
(A member of Struik New Holland Publishing (Pty) Ltd)
Cornelis Struik House
80 McKenzie Street
Cape Town 8001

Reg No: 54/00965/07

First published in 2000
10 9 8 7 6 5 4 3 2

Editors Susannah Coucher, Sean Fraser
Designer Robert House, Tracey Carstens
Cover designer Beverley Dodd
Illustrators David Thorpe
Consultant Charles Griffiths

Reproduction by Unifoto (Pty) Ltd, Cape Town
Printed and bound by CTP Book Printers

ISBN 1 86872 511 1